# ETHNIC FOODS
# OF
# HAWAI'I

by
Ann Kondo Corum

With
Illustrations by the Author
And Foreword by
Nino J. Martin

THE BESS PRESS
Box 22388
Honolulu, Hawai'i 97822

Executive Editor: Ann Rayson
Design and Typography: Richard Wirtz

**Library of Congress Cataloging in Publication Data**

CATALOG CARD NO.: 83-70358

Corum, Ann Kondo
Ethnic Foods of Hawai'i

Includes, Glossary, Bibliography, Index
Honolulu, Hawai'i: Bess Press

176 pages

Second Printing   1984
ISBN Number: 0-935848-21-5

iv

# Contents

# Foreword

Over the years I have presented demonstrations on many of the cuisines of the world on my television show. Many of my guests who have appeared on the program have been selected from the Hawaiian islands. The racial mix, representing many ethnic backgrounds, is one of the reasons Hawai'i is so rich in its cultural heritage and much of the reason my program has been so successful.

I am very pleased that Mrs. Corum has published this book, which represents the primary ethnic cultures of Hawai'i. It will share with the readers a sense of history and tradition as it reflects the cuisines and cooking methods of our island people.

Also, I believe this book will be extremely valuable to Hawai'i's youngsters, both in terms of learning the styles of the various ethnic cultures as well as helping better understand and appreciate their own ethnic origin.

To the non-resident, it is a new, refreshing and crisp approach in understanding the complex matrix that makes up the peoples of the islands.

I'm certain you will thank Mrs. Corum for her dedication and expertise in compiling this book.

Nino J. Martin
The International Chef®

# Preface

This book was conceived because of a need. In my years as a school librarian it seemed that, every year, students in Hawai'i's classrooms were researching the foods and food customs of the many ethnic groups that make up our state's population. While students had no trouble finding information on Japanese and Chinese food and customs, they found only limited information on the foods of other ethnic groups that are very much a part of our island state. Often, these materials were too complex or incomplete for the students to use, so I began formulating a book that would give students the information that they were looking for in a straightforward manner.

Over a period of several years I did research, collected clippings and recipes, and talked with many people about their ethnic foods and customs. The result of my study is this book, a book of food customs and holiday feasts with representative recipes from each ethnic group. It is hoped that this book, *Ethnic Foods of Hawai'i,* will be of interest to the general reader as well as students. I hope that it will introduce people of our islands to some facts they were unaware of and give visitors an overview of some food customs of this multi-racial state.

With the exception of the Hawaiians who were native to the islands, the Samoans who came from an American territory, and the Southeast Asians who came as refugees, the immigrant groups that came to Hawai'i all came as plantation laborers. Many came with the intention of working the duration of their contracts and returning to their native lands. They brought little with them except for memories of home which included traditions, customs, and native foods. Familiar dishes were recreated, sometimes with substitute ingredients. Races intermarried, creating a blend of customs and traditions in one family. Perhaps because Hawai'i is an island state and relatively isolated, the people hung on to their traditions. Thus, many of them survive today.

In this book the reader will see similarities in certain foods of different races. However, the chapters are arranged not by similar ethnic groups, but chronologically by the group's time of arrival in Hawai'i. The recipes included at the end of each chapter are only representative recipes and in no way are they intended to be a comprehensive selection. The reader should be aware that recipes are highly personal, that variations exist, and that substitution of ingredients is possible.

Many thanks go out to all who took the time to discuss their customs and culture with me and shared their recipes as well. My thanks also to my mother, Miyako Kondo, for her help in adapting the recipes, my husband, Van, and son, Ken, for their critical comments, and Dr. Ann Rayson for editing the manuscript. And thanks to the students of Prince David Kawananakoa Intermediate School for their questions and inspiration.

# Hawaiian

## Introduction

The most distinctive characteristic of Hawaiian food is that it is wholesome, pure, simply prepared food not covered with batter, sauces, or condiments. Seasoning is uncomplicated, salt and red pepper being the main seasonings.

The ancient Hawaiians who arrived in Hawai'i, circa 450 A.D., were physically well developed people even though grains and milk were unknown to them. They were entirely dependent on the land and the ocean for food. Their basic diet consisted of poi and taro, sweet potato, taro tops, bananas, seaweed, fish and seafood, pig, dog, and a domesticated fowl similar to chicken. These foods provided the Hawaiians with nutrients necessary for growth and health, making them one of the most advanced and robust of the Polynesian people.

It is interesting to note that even without refrigeration in a tropical climate, Hawaiians were able to preserve food for long periods. The acid in fermenting poi, a staple starch, allowed it to be preserved for several weeks. Meat such as pig was heavily salted and, therefore, kept from spoiling. Fish and other seafood were also preserved by salting and/or drying in the sun as was seaweed.

Today, people of Hawaiian and part-Hawaiian ancestry, as well as other ethnic groups of Hawai'i, enjoy the same nutritious and simply prepared foods that the ancient Hawaiians ate. In addition, dishes adopted from the New England missionaries such as stew, chowder, corned beef, salt salmon, and beef jerky,

1

have become what modern day islanders currently call *typical* Hawaiian food.

The best Hawaiian food, of course, is homemade. But there are several Hawaiian food restaurants in Hawai'i where one can taste traditional Hawaiian dishes. Also popular foods such as *kālua* pig, *laulau, poke,* and *haupia* are available prepared and packaged in large markets and specialty stores throughout the islands. For visitors to the islands, there are many hotels and tours which allow the diner to sample all kinds of typical Hawaiian *lū'au* food.

## Cooking Methods

The ancient Hawaiians had three major methods of cooking their food. Broiling, over hot coals *(kō'ala)* and over hot ashes *(pūlehu),* was one of the main methods. Bananas, breadfruit, and sweet potatoes were broiled in their skins while meats and fish were frequently wrapped in ti or banana leaves to keep their moisture while being broiled.

Boiling *(hākui, pūholo)* was another major cooking method. Because the Hawaiians did not have fireproof cooking utensils, they did not boil food directly over the fire. Instead, red hot stones were dropped into a calabash *('umeke)* along with the food to be cooked and some water. Fish and greens such as sweet potato leaves were most often prepared this way.

Roasting or steaming underground was by far the most important cooking method. The method was known as *kālua;* the underground oven known as *imu.* The preparation of an imu for today's lū'au is similar to the imu used by the ancient Hawaiians. First a hole was dug. Wood was placed in the hole along with kindling. Porous stones were heaped on top of the wood and the fire was lighted. When the stones reached a red hot stage, they were leveled and covered with a layer of crushed banana trunks. A layer of coarse grass or ti leaves was spread over the banana trunks. On this layer of greenery was placed the food to be cooked. The food was wrapped in ti or banana leaves, then covered with a coarse cloth such as "kapa" or coconut cloth. Today burlap bags are substituted for kapa. Dirt was sometimes heaped on top of the cloth. The kālua cooking process takes several hours, but food prepared in this manner is flavorful and succulent. Today most people cook their Hawaiian food on the stove simply because it is easier. But imu are still dug for special occasions.

Not really a cooking method, but rather a way of preserving fish and meat, was salting. Fish in particular was preserved this way. The fish were split or cut into strips, salted, and hung in sunshine to dry. Dried fish and poi remain two of the Hawaiian favorites even today. Many families in Hawai'i now have screened drying boxes in which they hang fish, octopus, and squid to dry in the sun.

## Kapu Relating to Food and Eating

Food and eating habits among the ancient Hawaiians were dictated by a system of restriction called kapu. The kapu system, based on prohibition and restraint, kept people obedient. It kept commoners obedient to the high priests and chiefs; it separated men from women. Kapu touched almost every aspect of the daily lives of Hawaiians.

The kapu system dominated the eating habits of the ancient Hawaiians. Men and women were not allowed to eat together. As in other Polynesian societies, men were considered almost sacred; women profane. In ancient Hawai'i men were definitely the dominant sex. Men and women were separated because they came under the jurisdiction of different classes of gods. Men ate in the presence of male gods to whom they had been dedicated as children; women ate in the presence of their family gods. Men and women had separate eating houses. Men ate in a house called the *hale mua* and women ate in a house called the *hale 'aina*. Women were not allowed into the eating area of men, although men were allowed to enter the eating area of women. As soon as boys were weaned from their mothers, they were not allowed to eat with women. Foods such as pork, most bananas, coconuts, certain kinds of fish such as *ulua* and *kūmū,* and turtle—foods offered to male gods in sacrifice—were forbidden to women. If a woman was caught eating these forbidden foods, she was put to death.

In ancient Hawai'i men were responsible for food preparation. Food for men and women was kept completely separate; that is, a man could not prepare one batch of poi and divide it between himself and his wife. He had to pound one batch for himself and another for his wife.

These kapu dictated the daily lives of Hawaiians until Liholiho (Kamehameha II), convinced by his father's favorite wife, Kaahumanu, and his mother, Keopuolani, broke the kapu on eating by eating with the women. This simple act was the beginning of *ai noa* or free eating, and was a drastic change in Hawaiian culture.

## Meat/Fish

Chicken, pig, dog, and fish were the main sources of meat for the early Hawaiians. Of these, fish was the main source of protein. The ancient Hawaiians fished in the ocean for most of their fish, but they also constructed fishponds and raised fish in these. Fish was sometimes eaten raw, but it was usually broiled whole over coals, wrapped in ti leaves and put on hot coals, or steamed by dropping hot stones into a calabash containing the fish and some water. Fish was also dried in the sun or preserved by salting. In addition to fish, other sea creatures such as turtles, sea urchins, limpets ('opihi), and other shellfish were used as food.

Fishermen were highly respected and had to go through many stages to prepare for their occupation. Many religious ceremonies were connected with fishing, as were kapu. There were numerous methods of fishing and different equipment for catching various fish. Most important, Hawaiian fishermen observed conservation of fishing grounds so as not to deplete their important source of food. They had respect for and knowledge of the sea and its resources.

Chickens, pigs, and dogs were considered a sign of wealth by the early Hawaiians. These were commonly fattened and saved for special feasts or religious ceremonies or for special visitors. Pig in particular was important as a ceremonial food. It, like coconuts and bananas, was forbidden food for women. Men ate pig only after it had been first offered to the gods and the gods had taken their share. The Hawaiian dog, which was raised for food, was probably a terrier-like animal. No description is possible because only its teeth remain.

Pigs and dogs were cooked in the imu. The Hawaiians did not eat poorly cooked meat. If it was not well done, the meat was used in laulau and cooked again or placed in calabashes with hot stones for further cooking. Chickens were also cooked in the imu. They were also prepared with lū'au leaves and coconut milk in the calabash with hot stones. In addition to chickens, the ancient Hawaiians utilized many varieties of wild fowl for food. Among them were the Hawaiian goose (nene), mudhen ('alae), wild duck *(kōloa)*, and plover *(kōlea)*.

Hawaiian food today, particularly food for special occasions, is very similar to the food of the ancient Hawaiians. 'Opihi and raw fish mixed with seaweed (poke) remain popular today. Laulau and kālua pig are cooked in the imu for lū'au. Chicken lū'au and fish wrapped in ti leaves are also popular. While kālua pig is usually cooked in the imu for a lū'au, simplified cooking methods are often used to prepare other foods, and there are even recipes for oven kālua pig which simulates the flavor of imu-cooked pig. Lū'au food can be completely prepared in the home on the stove and in the oven so that it can be enjoyed not only for special feasts, but for everyday.

### Poi and Taro

Poi—thick, grey, and paste-like—is the staple starch of Hawaiians. Poi is to the Hawaiian as rice is to the Oriental. To Hawaiians no celebration is complete without poi.

Poi is made from taro, one of the world's oldest cultivated crops. Known as "kalo" to the ancient Hawaiians, it was carried to Hawai'i by the Polynesians from the south. There are several varieties of taro. The bulbous underground corm of the taro plant is potato-like with a brown fibrous outer skin and grey, pink, or purple insides. The taro corm can be boiled, roasted, steamed, ground into flour, or sliced thin and fried into chips as well as pounded into poi. Ancient Hawaiians steamed taro in the imu. After steaming, the corm was peeled and eaten or sliced and dried in the sun. Dried, it could be preserved for a long period of time and used for food on long trips. The spinach-like leaves of the taro plant, called lū'au, can be cooked and added to other dishes or wrapped in ti-leaf packets with fish, pork, or chicken (laulau) and steamed. Taro cannot be eaten raw. Both the corm and leaves must be thoroughly cooked because the corms, stems, and leaves contain oxalic crystals that irritate the mouth until they are broken down in the cooking process.

While taro is cultivated throughout the South Pacific, the Hawaiians developed and perfected poi. Poi consists of cooked taro corms, mashed with water, and allowed to ferment. The degree of fermentation determines its flavor. Fresh poi is referred to as "sweet poi" while poi which has been allowed to ferment a few days is called "sour poi."

Nutritionally, poi is a starch, low in fat and protein, containing vitamin B, phosphorous, and calcium. It is lower in calories than rice (1 cup of poi contains 161 calories; 1 cup of cooked rice contains 248 calories). It has been praised as a health food. Many babies and elderly people unable to tolerate other foods have survived on a poi diet. In Hawai'i, many infants start eating poi as their first solid food.

Locally, poi is sold in markets in plastic bags. It is enjoyed by many ethnic groups, not only those of Hawaiian ancestry. People enjoy taro and poi in many different ways. Taro cakes, taro puffs, *kūlolo* (taro and coconut milk pudding), and poi bread are some of the ways in which taro and poi are used.

Poi and taro were culturally significant in the ancient Hawaiian's life. Taro was sacred for it was considered the elder brother of man. It was believed that the taro plant came from the eldest son of the god Wakea and the goddess Ho'ohuku-ka-lani. The child died and was buried. From its body arose a taro plant. The plant's stem was called Haloa. Later, another child was born to the god and goddess and was called Haloa, for the stalk of the taro. This second child is believed to be the origin of all mankind.

Family relationships are described in words synonymous with taro plants. 'Ohana, even today, refers to a social unit of family or relatives; 'ohana also refers to the offshoots of the taro corm, a source of life. The 'ohana, in turn, is tied to the 'aina, or the land which feeds it.

**Fruit**

Many varieties of tropical fruit are associated with Hawai'i today; however, most of the fruit, like other food plants, was brought to the islands from central Polynesia and elsewhere. Among the fruits indigenous to Hawai'i are berries such as 'akala (wild raspberry) and 'ōhelo berry.

Bananas (mai'a) and coconuts (niu) were important fruits to the early Hawaiians. Bananas are usually propagated by rhizomes, or bulb-like root stalks which run horizontally to the ground. When the early Polynesians migrated to Hawai'i they brought with them banana rhizomes and cultivated them for food. When white men first came to Hawai'i they found that the Hawaiians had 50 to 70 varieties of bananas. The varieties of bananas commonly seen today, such as Chinese, bluefield, and ice cream bananas, were introduced to the islands during the 19th century.

The original Hawaiian bananas were more of a cooking variety. Bananas are a good source of carbohydrate, a fair source of vitamin A, riboflavin, and niacin. Certain varieties provide a fair source of vitamin C. Bananas were considered an important food and were offered to gods and high chiefs at ceremonial feasts. Some varieties were kapu or forbidden fruit to women.

When the missionaries arrived in Hawai'i they found coconuts growing in the islands. These coconuts were small in size and of inferior quality, but nevertheless, they played an important role in the ancient Hawaiian's diet and daily life. The leaves were used in thatching houses and making baskets. Midribs of the leaves were made into brooms and snares. Coconut fiber was used for strainers and for making sandals. The soft meat of young coconuts, commonly known as "spoon meat," was fed to babies. Mature coconuts provided coconut milk, oil for liniment, hair oil, and light. Coconut shells were used as containers, hula rattles, and tools. The original coconuts, like bananas, were introduced to Hawai'i by migrating Polynesians. The many varieties of coconuts growing in the islands today were later arrivals that were introduced to the islands during the 19th century.

A coconut is considered mature when its husk begins to turn brown and the meat has reached maximum thickness. Usually when it reaches this point, it falls off the tree. Coconuts with their husks removed can be bought in island markets. The nut must be pierced through its "eyes" and the liquid drained. Then the nut should be tapped along its middle until the shell cracks open. The meat can then be grated. Ancient Hawaiians had coconut graters made out of 'opihi or cowrie shells. Hawaiians

and Samoans today have a similar grater which allows for grating of the coconut meat without removing it from the shell. The grater is usually made out of steel about 9 inches by 2 inches with curved teeth for grating on one end. The grater may be attached to a chair or a stool. Sitting on the stool, the person scrapes the halves of coconut (still in the shell) over the grater and the grated meat falls into a pan placed below it. Coconut meat can also be removed from its shell, its brown skin peeled, then grated in a food processor or with a conventional hand grater. Because of the time and labor involved, many people today use packaged grated coconut which, of course, does not have the flavor of fresh coconut. Coconut milk is easily prepared from fresh coconuts (see recipe section), but it is also available in cans or in the frozen food section of local markets.

Breadfruit 'ulu was also an important fruit to the ancient

Hawaiians. It too was brought by migrating Polynesians. Breadfruit is high in carbohydrate and is a fairly good source of calcium. It also provides vitamin C and riboflavin. Ancient Hawaiians most frequently baked unpeeled breadfruit in the imu. Today it is cooked in the oven. Breadfruit was sometimes used as a substitute for taro. Used in this way it was steamed in the imu, peeled, and cored. It was then mashed with a little water to form poi (poi 'ulu). Another way of preparing it is to add coconut milk to ripe breadfruit instead of water. The mixture is then wrapped in ti leaves and cooked in an imu or oven.

Although pineapple is always associated with Hawai'i, it too is not a native fruit. It was not known to the ancient Hawaiians. Pineapple is a native of South America and the circumstances of its actual introduction to the islands is not known. However, it is surmised that it came to Hawai'i through Spaniards who brought the fruit from South America during the early 1800s. Today pineapple growing and canning is one of the significant industries of Hawai'i.

Pineapple is a good source of natural sugar and thiamine and a fair source of calcium. It is most frequently served fresh in slices or chunks; however, it is also made into jams and preserves, and used in desserts and in salads. Pineapples are usually sweeter during the summer months. Unlike many fruits, pineapple does not increase in sweetness after it is picked because it does not store starch that can be converted into sugar. Instead, the sugar is in the leaves of the plant and is transferred to the fruit. Therefore, color and size alone are not always dependable guides for picking out a sweet pineapple.

Papaya, another fruit associated with Hawai'i, was also introduced to the islands in the 1880s. The melon-like papaya varies in size and shape. While it is usually eaten ripe as a breakfast fruit or in fruit salads, green papaya is used as a vegetable with a texture and flavor similar to that of squash. Papayas are found in all local markets, although their flavor and quality vary with the season of the year and rainfall.

Guava, the yellow, round fruit known for its juice, is another non-native fruit which has been associated with Hawai'i. Guavas grow wild in the islands. They are now cultivated commercially on a small scale, but are not offered for sale at the markets. Canned or frozen guava juice and guava jam and jelly are available at any store. Guava juice is a good substitute for orange juice because it is rich in vitamin C. Frozen guava juice concentrate can be used for baking pies and cakes.

Only some of the fruits popular in Hawai'i have been mentioned here. Other fruits of Hawai'i include passion fruit, mango, avocado, and mountain apple.

### Vegetables

Green vegetables were not a large part of the Hawaiian diet. However the heart shaped leaf of the taro plant (lū'au) was and still is the most popular green in Hawaiian cookery. When cooked, it is much like spinach and is used in making laulau and chicken lū'au. Lū'au leaves are now packaged and sold in most markets in Hawai'i.

The sweet potato ('uala) ranked next to the taro as the second most important staple among the early Hawaiians. It was

cultivated in the dry lands not suitable for growing taro. Sweet potatoes were cooked in the imu and eaten as is or they were sometimes mashed and mixed with water and eaten as sweet potato poi. Today sweet potatoes are most frequently baked (in oven or imu) or boiled. The tender leaves of the plant are usually boiled and eaten as greens. Hawaiians also made a kind of beer out of fermented sweet potato called 'uala 'awa'awa. Only certain varieties containing much sugar in the tubers were used. The cooked potatoes were mashed, mixed with water, and allowed to ferment in barrels for three or four days.

Yams (uhi) were also utilized by early Hawaiians, but to a lesser degree than sweet potatoes. Similar to sweet potatoes, yams were prepared the same way. However, their mealy texture made them unsuitable for mashing into poi.

In addition to taro, sweet potato, and yam tops, leaves and shoots of many wild native plants were cooked and eaten as vegetables. These included the pith of the tree fern (*hāpuʻu*), fern shoots, and shoots of an herb called *pōpolo*.

**Seaweed** (*Limu*)

Limu or seaweed was a versatile and valuable food for the ancient Hawaiians. Because they did not eat many leafy vegetables, seaweed took the place of vegetables in their diet. Seaweed provides many vitamins, including A, B-complex, D, E, and K as well as many trace minerals. It is also a good source of roughage or fiber. Certain varieties are high in protein.

Many different varieties of limu were eaten by the Hawaiians. Depending on the variety, limu was eaten fresh, dried, or preserved with salt. In salt, it could be preserved for a long period of time. Limu was also used in combination with other foods such as octopus, fish, and poi. It was also used in soups and baked with fish or chicken in the imu. One variety of limu called *limu kohu* was cleaned and pounded with a mortar and pestle to make a relish. It was then pinched between thumb and fingers and eaten in combination with other foods.

Limu is sold today in markets when it is available. Among the most popular varieties are *limu manauea*, commonly known as *ogo*, limu kohu, and *limu ʻeleʻele*. Depending on the variety, it is sold fresh in plastic bags or salted in small containers. One can also gather limu in many places in the islands along the shore or along reefs. Limu must be thoroughly washed to remove sand and rock as well as tiny animals that live on it.

There are numerous ways of preparing limu. Ways of preparing it are similar to the methods of the ancient Hawaiians. It may be added to fish or shellfish, added to meat or fowl and then baked, or made into pickles and relishes. Limu can be eaten raw; however, many island cooks today wilt it with hot water before using it in recipes.

### Feasts and Celebrations

Ancient Hawaiian feasts and celebrations were mainly religious in nature. A feast followed sacred ceremonies such as the birth of a child, marriage, or death. When a piece of work was completed, such as the building of a canoe or a new house, a feast followed. The feast was supposed to thank the god (akua) or guardian spirit ('aumakua) that helped make the work a success. 'Aumākua were present for anything a person did. They were honored at any feast with food placed on an altar. The Hawaiians believed that the 'aumākua ate the food and enjoyed the feast.

Today in Hawai'i not only Hawaiians, but many nationalities, have a lū'au or feast to celebrate occasions such as marriage, graduation, or a child's birthday. And it is not uncommon to celebrate the building of a new home.

A thanksgiving celebration known as the Makahiki was an important celebration for the ancient Hawaiians. It spanned four months for the ali'i, beginning in October or November and ending in February or March. The Makahiki was mainly a time of paying tribute to Lono, the god of peace and plenty. During the Makahiki people did not work as usual. It was a time of peace and religious ceremonies as well as a time of feast and celebration. People made special offerings to the king and to Lono. Gifts, including taro, pig, sweet potatoes, kapa, and mats were placed on the altar for Lono. These were to thank him for a year of prosperity, but they also served as a tax paid to the king.

Hawaiians do not celebrate Makahiki today, but they, like other ethnic groups in the islands, celebrate traditional Thanksgiving Day as well as Christmas, New Year's Day, and Easter with friends, family and good food.

# Coconut Milk

COCONUT MILK is the liquid that is extracted from the meat of the mature coconut after soaking it in boiling milk or water. If using fresh coconuts, choose a coconut that is mature, but not dry. After removing the husk, crack the nut with a hammer and remove the meat. Peel off the brown skin; grate the meat by hand or process in a food processor. When grated, an average coconut produces approximately 3 cups of meat. If fresh coconuts are not available, use dried, unsweetened coconut which is available in health food or Oriental grocery stores.

To obtain coconut milk from the grated coconut, use 1 cup of whole milk to 1 cup of grated coconut. Scald the milk in a saucepan; place coconut in the milk. Stir, remove from heat, and let stand until cool. Strain this mixture through a sieve lined with cheesecloth or a thin dish towel. Squeeze out as much liquid as possible. Refrigerate. This milk may also be frozen for future use. Coconut milk is also available frozen in cans at most local markets.

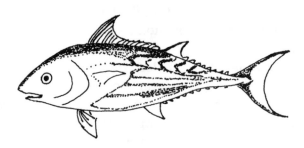

# Aku Poke
## Raw Fish with Seaweed

**Serves 6**

    1 lb. raw fish (aku or ahi)
    Hawaiian salt to taste
    limu manauea (ogo), about 1 pint
    1 red chili pepper, seeds removed

Cube raw fish into 1-inch squares. Add salt to taste. Clean limu well, rinsing in water several times. Chop limu into 1-inch pieces. Combine fish and limu and mix with hands. Add pepper. Chill until ready to serve.

**Note:** This may be prepared with octopus (poke he'e).

# Lomi Salmon

**Serves 4-6**

1 lb. salted salmon
1 onion, chopped
3 large tomatoes, diced

3 stalks green onions, chopped
3 cubes of ice, cracked

Soak salted salmon in cold water for 1 hour. If salmon is very salty, repeat process. Remove skin and bones and shred salmon with fingers. Place in a bowl and add tomatoes and onions. Chill; add crushed ice just before serving.

**Note:** Lomi in Hawaiian means to squeeze, crush, mash fine.

# Pipi Kaula
## Hawaiian Style Jerky

2 lbs. flank steak
¾ cup soy sauce
2 Tbsp. Hawaiian salt
1½ Tbsp. sugar

1 clove garlic, minced
1 piece ginger, crushed
1 red chili pepper, crushed
(optional)

Cut beef into strips 1½ inches wide. Combine all other ingredients and soak beef in the sauce overnight. If you have a drying box, place the meat in hot sun for two days, bringing it in at night. If drying in the oven, set oven to 175 degrees. Place meat on a rack such as a cake cooling rack. Place rack on a cookie sheet and dry meat in oven for 7 hours. Keep in refrigerator.

# Oven Kālua Pig

2 Tbsp. Hawaiian salt
¼ c. soy sauce
1 tsp. Worcestershire sauce
2 cloves garlic, crushed

1 piece ginger, crushed
1 Tbsp. liquid smoke
4-5 lbs. pork roast
ti or banana leaves

Mix together salt, soy sauce, Worcestershire sauce, garlic, ginger and liquid smoke. Place pork on several ti or banana leaves. Rub with seasoning and let stand 1 hour. Fold leaves over to wrap the pork. Wrap the leaf enclosed pork in foil. Place in a baking pan and bake in a 325 degree oven for 4-5 hours. Unwrap and shred the meat.

# Mahimahi in Coconut Milk

**Serves 4**

4 mahimahi fillets
1½ cup coconut milk
1 small onion, chopped
1 small green pepper, chopped
1 tomato, diced

salt to taste
cayenne pepper to taste
1 Tbsp. butter
1 Tbsp. flour

Place coconut milk, onions, green pepper, and a little salt in a pan. Bring to a gentle boil and place the fish in it. Poach fish until it is done; remove from the coconut milk and place on serving dish and keep warm. Simmer the coconut milk. Mix softened butter with flour and add to the coconut milk, stirring to prevent lumps. Add tomatoes, salt and cayenne pepper to taste. Simmer 2-3 minutes. Pour sauce over the fish.

**Variation:** Other fish such as mullet or 'ōpakapaka may be substituted.

# Chicken Lūau

**Serves 4-6**

2 lbs. chicken
2 Tbsp. oil
2 cloves garlic, crushed
2 c. coconut milk
2½ c. water
2 lbs. taro leaves (lū'au)
1½ tsp. salt

Prepare fresh coconut milk or use prepared, canned coconut milk. Cut chicken into bite sized pieces. Heat oil; add crushed garlic. Brown chicken. Sprinkle with 1 tsp. salt and add 1 c. water. Simmer until chicken is tender. Wash taro leaves; remove tough stems and ribs. Place leaves in pan with 1½ c. water and ½ tsp. salt. Simmer, partially covered, for 1 hour. Drain and squeeze water out. Drain chicken; combine with the lū'au leaves. Add coconut milk and bring to a boil. Serve immediately.

**Note:** Fresh spinach may be substituted if lū'au is not available.

# Laulau

**Makes 6**

18 taro leaves (lū'au); more if leaves are small
2 lbs. pork butt, cut in 6 pieces
1 lb. salted butterfish, cut in 6 pieces
6 chicken thighs (optional)
12 ti leaves

Wash and prepare each ti leaf by cutting the stiff rib partially through and stripping it off the leaf. Wash taro leaves and remove stem and tough veins. For each laulau take 3 large taro leaves, overlapping them, and place a piece of pork, butterfish, and chicken on it. Fold leaves to form a bundle. Place laulau on a ti leaf and wrap tightly. Wrap another ti leaf around it in the opposite direction. Tie with string. Steam laulau in a covered steamer for 3½-4 hours, or cook in a pressure cooker for 35-40 minutes at 15 lbs. pressure.

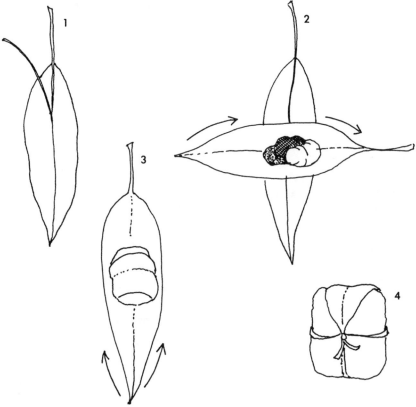

# Chicken Long Rice

**Serves 4-6**

1 chicken, about 3 lbs.
water
½" slice of ginger, crushed
1 bundle long rice, soaked in water to soften
salt to taste
3 stalks green onions

Place chicken in a large pot and cover with water. Add ginger and bring to a boil; lower heat and simmer about 45 minutes to an hour, or until meat falls away from the bones. Remove chicken from broth and discard bones. Return chicken to broth and add long rice. Simmer until about half of the broth is absorbed by the long rice. Season with salt and add green onions just before serving.

This is a popular dish served at modern Hawaiian lūʻau.

# Poi Bread

**Makes 2 loaves**

1 bag poi (1 lb.)
2 c. flour
2 tsp. cinnamon
2 tsp. baking soda
3 eggs, slightly beaten
2 tsp. vanilla
½ c. shredded coconut

¾ c. water
1 c. sugar
½ tsp. nutmeg
1 tsp. salt
1 c. oil
½ c. chopped nuts
½ c. raisins

Mix poi and water; blend well. In a large bowl combine flour, sugar, cinnamon, nutmeg, baking soda, and salt. Combine eggs, oil, and vanilla; add to flour mixture. Stir in poi; add nuts, coconut, and raisins. Pour into two greased loaf pans and bake for 45 minutes at 350 degrees.

# Kūlolo
## Taro Pudding

**Serves 8**

    4 c. taro, grated          1 c. coconut milk
    ¾ c. brown sugar           2 ti leaves
    1 c. honey

Mix all ingredients together. Line a bread loaf with foil. Put the ti leaves on the foil, cutting to fit the pan. Pour pudding into the pan and cover top with foil. Bake 2 hours in 400 degree oven. Remove foil during the last half hour to allow pudding to brown.

**Note:** Kūlolo was originally prepared with grated taro and shredded coconut. It was wrapped in ti leaves and baked in the imu.


# Haupia
## Coconut Pudding

**Serves 9**

    3 c. coconut milk
    6 Tbsp. cornstarch
    6 Tbsp. sugar

Mix cornstarch and sugar together. Add enough coconut milk to make a smooth paste. Heat the remaining coconut milk to boiling and slowly add the cornstarch paste. Lower heat and cook until mixture thickens, stirring to prevent lumps. Pour into an 8 inch square pan and chill. Cut into squares.

**Note:** Originally haupia was prepared with arrowroot (pia) mixed with coconut cream. It was wrapped in ti leaves and baked in the imu.

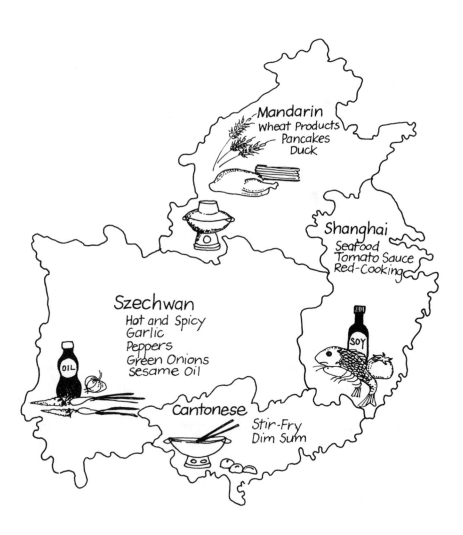

Mandarin
Wheat Products
Pancakes
Duck

Shanghai
Seafood
Tomato Sauce
Red-Cooking

Szechwan
Hot and Spicy
Garlic
Peppers
Green Onions
Sesame Oil

Cantonese
Stir-Fry
Dim Sum

# Chinese

## Introduction

Chinese food has long been one of the favorite ethnic foods among Americans. Along with French food, it is known as one of the great cuisines of the world. The many sauces and condiments in Chinese food create delicate and subtle differences in the flavor of ordinary food. Perhaps this is the source of its appeal to many people. Chinese people place a great importance on food and are often said to be preoccupied with eating. This delight in eating is apparent in the wide variety of their dishes.

The Chinese arrived in Hawai'i to work as plantation laborers in 1852. These early immigrants were predominantly from the southern part of China, around Canton. Hence, in Hawai'i the Cantonese style of cooking predominates, although currently the northern style of cooking is making itself known through numerous restaurants which specialize in northern cuisine.

Basically, there are four regional styles of Chinese cooking. They are Mandarin, from Peking in the northern part of China; Szechwan, from the central plains; Shanghai from the eastern coast; and Cantonese, from the south. Mandarin cuisine is called the gourmet cuisine of China. It can be characterized as light and mildly seasoned. Peking duck, Mongolian fire pot, and Mandarin pancakes are popular dishes from this region. Szechwan cooking is characterized by hot chili peppers, garlic, and sesame oil. It is the spiciest style of Chinese cooking. Shanghai, a cosmopolitan city situated at the mouth of the Yangtze River, was at one time an important trading center with much foreign influence. Its cuisine shows this influence in the use of tomato sauce, milk, and milk products. Rich brown sauce and reddish soy sauce gravy are characteristic of the cooking of Shanghai. Seafood is the main ingredient in Shanghai cuisine. Cantonese cooking is the style most Americans are familiar with, for the Cantonese were the first to leave China and establish restaurants elsewhere. Stir-fried foods, sweet-sour dishes, and "dim sum" (dumplings) are characteristic Cantonese fare.

There are many similarities between Japanese and Chinese foods. Like the Japanese, Chinese cooks place emphasis on the pleasing appearance of a dish. And as in Japanese meals, many dishes make up the meal, rather than one main dish. Rice is a staple with the Chinese as it is with the Japanese and Koreans; however, the Chinese have an equal fondness for noodles as a staple starch. Like the Japanese, the Chinese always serve hot tea with the meal.

There are hundreds of Chinese restaurants in Hawai'i, ranging from family style simple restaurants and take-out counters to elegant restaurants with specialty dishes served on porcelain dinnerware. Each chef has his own style of cooking, and a lover of Chinese cuisine learns to appreciate the subtle differences in each restaurant's style.

In Hawai'i it is not difficult to find the spices, sauces, condiments, and specialty ingredients necessary to cook Chinese food. While some ingredients can only be found in Chinatown, most of the basic ingredients can be found in any large supermarket.

**Cooking Methods**

Typically, Chinese cooking, like other Oriental cooking, involves maximum time in preparation and not much time in actual cooking. Meats and vegetables must be sliced thin. Often meat is soaked in a marinade. There are certain cooking utensils which are specifically made for cooking Chinese food, but they are not necessities. Most kitchen tools can be adapted for cooking Chinese food. A cutting board, either wooden or plastic and a sharp knife, however, are absolute necessities. The Chinese cleaver, which seems clumsy to Western cooks, is used by Chinese cooks for every cutting purpose from slicing meat to chopping vegetables. This tool is a wise investment for anyone who does much Chinese cooking.

Stir-frying is the most typical method of preparing Chinese food. The main idea in this method is to cook the food evenly on a high heat very quickly to retain tenderness in the meat and crispness, color, and nutrients in the vegetables. While a Chinese wok is recommended, a flat bottomed cast iron skillet or even an electric frying pan will serve the purpose. The wok is recommended because its curved sides allow for a larger cooking area

and it retains heat well. For stir-frying, a small amount of oil is heated in the pan before any food is added. To be successful with this method, the cook must have an understanding of the foods being cooked and must be aware of how long it takes each ingredient to reach its desired consistency. Firm vegetables such as carrots are added first, tender ones such as green onions last. Stir-frying is very simple once the cook understands the nature of each ingredient and how to control the pan's temperature.

Steaming is another method of cooking Chinese foods. The economical Chinese devised a bamboo steamer which allows many foods to be steamed at the same time by stacking one

circular tray above the other. Using this method, fuel is saved and many dishes can be cooked at the same time. Foods that are often steamed include fish, fowl, meats and dumplings called dim sum.

Roasting is primarily a method the Chinese use to prepare poultry and pork. The meat is seasoned and/or marinated, then roasted on a rack or on a spit. The finished roast has a crisp skin and appetizing color. Pot roasting is also popular, *kau yuk* or pot roast pork, being the most widely known dish. Chinese pot roasting is like braising. The meat is generally cooked slowly in a sauce, usually of a soy sauce base. Foods cooked this way have a rich, reddish brown color, and are often referred to as "red-cooked."

Deep frying in hot oil is another method of Chinese cooking. Meats are either marinated or coated with batter before frying. Generally, the batter used by the Chinese is not as light and delicate as the batter used by the Japanese for tempura. Often foods that are deep fried are served with a sweet-sour sauce as in sweet-sour shrimp or pork.

### Seasonings

Chinese cooks utilize seasonings in subtle ways; they try to accentuate natural flavors rather than conceal them. Relatively few spices are used in Chinese cookery, but when they are used they make extraordinary differences in otherwise ordinary foods.

Besides soy sauce and soybean derivatives, which are the most widely used seasonings in Chinese cooking, there are a variety of seasonings that are relatively unknown to Western

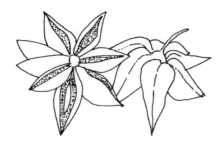

cooks. Among the popular spices used is five-spice powder. This consists of a blend of star anise, cloves, fennel, cinnamon, and Szechuwan peppercorns. This spice, frequently used in red-cooked meat and poultry, gives food a pungent flavor. Star anise, a small, star-shaped fruit, in dried form is used in stewed meats and poultry and also eggs. Its flavor is similar to licorice.

Flavored oils, such as chili oil and sesame oil, are also used. These oils are used sparingly as seasoning rather than cooking oils. Dried orange or tangerine peel is sometimes used to season stewed meat dishes. Dried red chilies, dried lotus seeds, dried dates, and sesame seeds are also frequently used to enhance dishes. Plum sauce, a sweet, spicy sauce, is used as a dipping sauce.

Ginger root also adds flavor to many Chinese dishes. When using ginger, one should remember to use it sparingly so that it does not overpower the other ingredients, about an ⅛ inch thick piece suffices. Seasonings are an important part of Chinese cookery; however, one must be careful to use them only sparingly.

### Soybean and Bean Products

Chinese cooks utilize soybean products extensively. They use bean curd, known as *dow foo* in Chinese, but more commonly known as tofu, in all forms—fresh, dried, and preserved. In addition, they are fond of fresh soft tofu which is sold in one pound cartons in Chinatown. This tofu is soft and smooth like yogurt and is scooped up and eaten on hot rice.

Tofu and tofu products have always been used in the Orient as an important source of protein. The Chinese refer to tofu as "meat without bones." While tofu and tofu products do not contain as much protein by weight as meat, fish or poultry, they contribute substantial amounts of protein, especially if used in combination with small amounts of meat, nuts, seeds, or grains. Four ounces of tofu contains as much protein as a large egg. Its calcium content equals that of milk and it is low in fat and carbohydrate. One block of tofu contains about 351 calories.

Soybean products are widely used in Chinese seasonings. Plain soy sauce is a standard seasoning. Thick soy sauce, a dark, stronger flavored soy sauce which is like molasses in consistency, is used to flavor some dishes. Other soybean based sauces include bean paste and hoisin sauce, which has a sweet, spicy flavor.

Fermented black beans are sometimes used in place of salt to add an unusual flavor to meat, seafood, and poultry. Sweetened bean paste is used for filling sweet buns such as moon cakes. Beans are also used to make "cellophane noodles" or "long rice." These are names given to dried, transparent noodles made out of mung bean starch. The clear, colorless noodles are soaked in water, then added to various dishes.

### Meats

Pork and chicken are preferred by the Chinese. Beef, perhaps because it is so scarce in China, is used sparingly. Many of the dishes we eat in restaurants and cook in homes today which use beef have been adapted from the original use of pork in the dish.

In stir-fry recipes, the meat is sliced in thin strips in order to cook quickly. Generally, any tender cut of steak may be used; however, flank steak is a favorite cut of Chinese cooks. When pork is used in stir-fry dishes, any boneless pork filet or even pork chops may be sliced thin and used. Pork butt and pork loin are used for roasting and making *char siu,* a sweet flavored roasted pork. The Chinese have a favorite spicy sausage called *lup chong.* It is used alone, steamed or fried, or it is mixed with other ingredients. Lup chong is often added to fried rice.

Chicken is a favorite meat among the Chinese and they have endless ways of preparing it. Chicken broth is an essential in many Chinese dishes and often is the basis of their clear soups to which other ingredients are added. Duck is another favorite fowl. Pressed duck and Peking duck are two notable Chinese dishes. However, cooking duck at home is not very successful because the cooking process is complicated.

Chinese use all parts of an animal in their cooking. Chicken feet, liver, gizzard, and skin are considered important. Pig's feet, intestines, and tripe (the lining of a cow's stomach) are also considered delicacies.


## Fish and Seafood

The Chinese are very fond of all seafood. Fish and shellfish are used fresh, dried, canned or frozen. Fishcake is popular too. Chinese fishcake is not the ready made *kamaboko* fishcake seen in local markets. Rather, it is scraped and pounded flesh of fish which resembles a smooth, grayish paste. Fishcake in this form is sold in local fish markets and larger supermarkets. It is often combined with ground pork, shrimp, water chestnuts, or bamboo shoots and made into steam rolls, stuffed into squash or peppers, dropped into hot soup, or made into dumplings and then stir-fried with vegetables.

Large, firm fleshed fish, such as sea bass or 'ōpakapaka (pink snapper) are cooked whole, either steamed, fried, or baked. Sometimes these fish are served with a sweet-sour or black bean sauce, but often they are merely garnished with chopped green onions, ginger, or Chinese parsley (*cilantro*).

Shrimp, lobster, squid, and scallops are considered delicacies. These are often stir-fried with vegetables to make a seafood chop suey or served with a sauce such as black bean sauce. Dried seafood is also popular. In the Chinese grocery one can find dried delicacies such as abalone, cuttlefish, jellyfish, scallops, shrimp, and shark's fin. These must first be soaked in water for a time ranging from twenty minutes to twenty-four hours, depending on the item.

The Chinese use seafood pastes (*harm har*) and oyster sauce as seasonings. These pastes are fermented shrimp or oysters and have a strong, fishy odor. Added to foods in small amounts, they add distinctive flavor.

## Eggs

The Chinese have some unusual ways of preparing eggs. Salted and preserved duck's eggs are a favorite. The famous "thousand year old eggs" are in reality only four or five months old. Duck eggs are coated with a paste of lime, clay, salt, and ashes. The chemical reaction of the paste on the raw egg turns it into a translucent, creamy textured egg. These eggs (hard boiled) are usually served as a first cold course of a meal. Fresh eggs are used to make fu young and are often added to soups.

Eggs are considered a symbol of good luck, happiness, and prosperity to Chinese people. Red dyed eggs are often distributed to friends by the family of a new born child, much like the custom of American parents giving away cigars.

## Vegetables

Vegetables tend to predominate over meat in Chinese food. In many dishes, meats are used more as a flavoring for vegetables rather than the principal ingredient of the dish. Because Chinese rarely used dairy products in China, they had to get protein, vitamins, calcium, and other minerals from other foods. Vegetables helped to supply these basic nutrients necessary for health.

Besides using soybeans to get many nutrients, the Chinese use many varieties of beans and peas. Among other popular vegetables are cabbages, including mustard, head cabbage, and Chinese cabbage (won bok), turnips, squash, broccoli, green

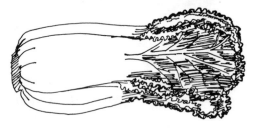

peppers, eggplants, and onions. In fact, there are very few vegetables that Chinese cooks do not use.

Because of their love of vegetables, Chinese of north China long ago perfected farming methods so that they could have fresh vegetables even through winter months. Their methods included planting varieties of vegetables that were resistant to cold, protecting crops with straw mats that could be removed on warm days, and planting on manure. Fresh produce to the Chinese has never been considered a luxury item, but rather a necessity.

Chinese do not have salads in the Western sense. However, cooked vegetables are never well done, and hence they retain their color, crispness, and vitamins. Crunchy textures and flavors of individual vegetables are maintained by using the stir-fry method. Vegetables are never boiled; Chinese cooks maintain that vegetables already contain much water so they should be stir-fried, then braised in their own juices.

Chinese people like to present their food artistically. For special occasions, chefs may carve intricate designs on a large winter melon (a kind of squash) which serves as a container as well as food. Soup is cooked inside the carved melon and it is served with pieces of scooped out squash. Fresh vegetables are also used decoratively. Flowers, birds, and gods are carved out of

vegetables such as carrots, turnips, radishes, and onions and used as decorations.

Vegetables are also pickled, salted, or dried and used in various ways. Salted and preserved mustard cabbage, known as "sin choy," is the most widely used. This vegetable, similar to the Japanese "tsukemono," is eaten as a relish or may be stir-fried with beef to create a flavorful dish. Salted and preserved turnip (chung choy) is used in small quantities to add flavor and texture to some dishes.

**Starches**

Rice is the staple starch among the Chinese. Boiled, steamed rice is always served with the meal. However, rice is used in other forms too. Rice flour is used to make various sweet cakes and dumplings. Rice is also used in Chinese soups such as the traditional "jook," a rice gruel with bits of chicken, pork, and vegetables. And we are all familiar with the ever popular fried rice.

Chinese are also fond of noodles. Noodles are known as *mein* or *min*. The range in form from thin, spaghetti-like noodles to wide, flat bands. Closely related to the noodles and made from the same water and flour base are the wrappers of skins for dumplings known as *won ton* and wrappers for egg rolls and spring rolls. The transparent, thin, "cellophane noodles" or "long rice" are made out of mung bean starch paste and sold in dry bundles. These dry noodles must be soaked in water before use.

Chinese cuisine from the north utilizes more wheat than cuisines from other areas of China. Because this area is more arid, it grows wheat rather than rice, and wheat and millet are staples of the people. Flour dumplings and pancakes are used as well as noodles. Mandarin pancakes, similar in texture and appearance to flour tortillas, are filled with stir-fried meats and vegetables as are buns made out of flour, water, and lard.

**Dim Sum**

Dim Sum, generally referred to as *manapua* in Hawai'i, is unique to Chinese cuisine. Dim sum is a general name given to a variety of dumplings, each having a specific name such as *char siu bao* (pork filled bun). Some varieties are baked; others are steamed or deep fried.

Dim sum outer coverings or wrappers can be made out of

glutinous rice flour (mochiko) or plain flour and water. Certain dim sum dough has shortening or lard in it, making a flaky, piecrust-like dumpling. Steamed dim sum has a soft, sticky texture while baked dim sum tends to have a texture like bread or rolls. Deep fried dim sum is made out of glutinous rice and is usually crisp on the outside and sticky on the inside. The dumplings are made in a variety of shapes and are filled with chopped shrimp, pork, vegetables, or sweets such as black sugar and coconut. There are many styles of dim sum from different regions of China, each with a unique flavor of its own.

Dim sum is not often made at home, but there are numerous restaurants and take-out shops that specialize in dim sum. In Hawai'i, this unique food can even be purchased from manapua trucks at various locations and is even served periodically for school lunches. Dim sum is popular for breakfast among the Chinese, but it is also eaten for lunch and snacks.

## Sweets

For Oriental people, the Chinese have a greater variety of sweets than do the Japanese or Koreans. While dessert, other than a light "sweet soup," is rarely served at the end of a Chinese meal, the Chinese have a variety of sweet cakes and pastries which are used primarily as festival foods. Some sweets are made specifically for occasions such as New Year's Day or the Moon Festival.

Generally, Chinese pastries are rich, flaky buns filled with either sweetened bean paste or salted eggs. Almond cookies are popular with Americans as well as Chinese. Candied fruits and vegetables are prepared for special occasions also, as is peanut-rice candy.

Some sweets such as gin tui (dumpling filled with black sugar) are deep fried in oil. Others such as sponge cake made out of rice and gau, a glutinous rice cake similar to the Japanese mochi, are steamed. Some of the older Chinese people still make their sweets at home, but generally the sweets are purchased at Chinese sweet shops in Chinatown.

## Tea

Tea is known as the national beverage of China. Many different kinds of teas are used, the three major types being green, oolong, and black. Many teas are combined with dried fruit peels or flowers to produce a distinctive flavor and fragrance. Jasmine and chrysanthemum teas are perhaps the two best known of the flavored teas. Tea is always served plain, with no milk or sugar.

Tea is not only a beverage to drink with one's meals. It has many social connotations. Tea is served to visitors in the home and at businesses. It is served with candied fruit and vegetables to New Year's visitors in the home. Because the tea plant cannot be transplanted and live, it is said that tea to the Chinese symbolizes fidelity. The offering of tea is found in almost all of the Chinese religious rites.

## Celebrations and Customs

Two main occasions which have remained with the Chinese in Hawai'i are Chinese New Year and the Moon Festival. The Chinese New Year does not fall on the first day of our calendar year. It is based on the lunar year, which is based on the cycles of the moon. The lunar year varies from year to year; however, it is bound to fall between January 20 and February 20 of any given year.

Like many Orientals the Chinese place great importance on the New Year. It is a time for new beginnings and hope for happiness and prosperity. Traditionally in China it was a time to clear all one's debts, clean house, pay respect to elders, and give gifts to friends. Thanks were given to dieties and offerings made to ancestral altars.

One of the traditional Chinese New Year's dishes is called jai or "monk's food." It is said that Buddhist monks used to beg for food from door to door. They were given mostly leftover vegetables, and hence, the creation of jai. The ingredients used in this dish vary from cook to cook. While the original jai was a strictly vegetarian dish, some cooks flavor their jai with oyster sauce, dried oysters, or chicken broth. Jai consists mainly of dry ingredients, many available only at New Year's and only at Chinese grocery stores. Fresh vegetables such as snow peas, carrots, and won bok (Chinese cabbage) are added for contrast in color and texture.

Several ingredients used in this dish have symbolic significance pertaining to good luck or happiness. Chinese are fond of a play on words, and many of the ingredients imply luck. For instance fat choy (algae) indicates wealth, Other ingredients frequently used include fungus and long rice for longevity, lotus seeds for fertility, mushrooms to welcome spring, and lily flower for much gold and good luck.

Chinese make a sticky glutinous rice flour cake like the Japanese mochi at New Year's. This sticky sweet cake, called gau, is usually topped by a single red preserved date. The stickiness of the gau symbolizes togetherness and the red date good luck (red is the good luck color). Also during the New Year celebration, special sweets such as candied fruits, lotus seeds, almond seeds, and watermelon seeds are offered to visitors in the home. The fruit and seeds signify fertility. The name for lotus seed is lien tzu, which means many sons. In general, Chinese New Year is a time of feasting on elaborate foods and a time of sharing joy.

The Moon Festival remains one of the important celebrations among the local Chinese. The moon goddess, Heng-O, celebrates her birthday traditionally on the fifteenth day of the eighth month of the lunar calendar year (mid autumn). In the old days, the Moon Festival coincided with the harvest season. Hence, the Moon Festival is a time to celebrate life and a time of thanksgiving.

Moon cakes are special to the Moon Festival. These cakes are available at local Chinese sweet shops in Chinatown and cost between $2.00 and $2.25 apiece. These cakes, made out of flour, sugar, and shortening, are filled with various fillings ranging

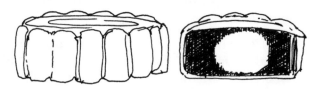

from coconut and fruit, to minced ham, and sweet bean paste. Usually a salted duck egg is tucked in the middle. Watermelon seeds and almonds are also tucked into moon cakes. The eggs symbolize joy as well as the golden moon, and it is said that those who eat moon cakes with seeds will be blessed with fertility.

There are several stories surrounding the moon cake. According to one Chinese legend, moon cakes freed China from invading Mongols during the 14th century. The Chinese were heavily guarded by Mongolians at every household and could not openly plan a revolution. During the Autumn Thanksgiving season, the Chinese ate moon cakes under the watchful eyes of the guards. But unknown to the guards, secret messages instructing the Chinese as to time and place of a revolution had been tucked inside each moon cake. The revolution was a success and Chinese rule returned. The salted duck egg tucked inside each moon cake is said to be a reminder of the secret messages of long ago.

# Won Bok and Pork Soup

**Serves 4**

| | |
|---|---|
| 1½ lbs. won bok | 1 tsp. sherry |
| ½ lb. ground pork | 2 tsp. salt |
| 2 Tbsp. chopped green onion | 2 cans (15oz.) chicken broth |
| small piece ginger, crushed | 1 can (6½ oz.) sliced |
| 1 egg, slightly beaten | mushrooms |

Cut won bok into 2-inch pieces. Combine pork, green onion, egg, ginger, sherry and ½ tsp. salt. Shape pork into 1-inch balls. Heat stock, add pork balls; simmer 20 minutes, covered. Add won bok, mushrooms, and remaining 1½ tsp. salt. Simmer 5 minutes.

# Won Ton

**Approximately 3 dozen**

| | |
|---|---|
| 1 lb. ground pork | ½ lb. Chinese fishcake |
| 1 tsp. sugar | 1 Tbsp. soy sauce |
| salt and pepper to taste | 6 water chestnuts, minced |
| 2 stalks green onion, chopped | |
| oil for frying | won ton wrappers |

Mix all ingredients together. Place a generous spoonful of the pork mixture in the middle of won ton wrapper. Dampen edges with water and form a triangle, pressing edges together with fingers. Pull the bottom corners of the triangle gently down below their base, overlap the tips of the two corners slightly, and pinch them together. Fry in hot oil until golden brown and crisp. Drain on paper towels.

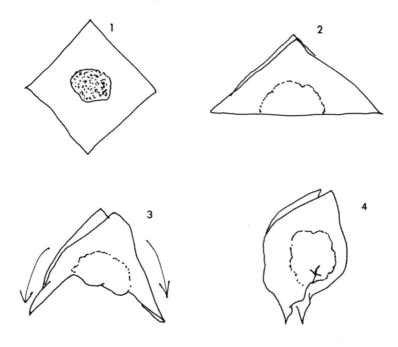

**Variation:** Won Ton may be cooked in chicken broth and served as a soup. Garnish the soup with green onions, Chinese cabbage, or mustard cabbage.

# Egg Fu Young

**Serves 4-6**

½ c. ham, slivered
½ c. water chestnuts, slivered
½ c. carrots, slivered
1 c. bean sprouts
4 eggs, slightly beaten
½ tsp. soy sauce

1 stalk celery, cut diagonally
  into thin pieces
2 stalks green onion, cut into
  ½ inch pieces
½ tsp. salt
¼ tsp. sugar

Stir fry ham and vegetables in a small amount of hot oil until tender but crisp. Remove from heat; cool. Season eggs with salt, soy sauce, and sugar. Mix in the vegetables and ham. Heat a little oil in pan. Drop 3 Tbsp. of egg mixture in at a time. Fry until brown on both sides over low heat.

**Variation:** Chopped shrimp may be used in place of ham.

# Char Siu

5 lb. pork butt, sliced
¾ c. sugar
red food coloring

2 Tbsp. Hawaiian salt
2 Tbsp. Hoi Sin Sauce

Marinate overnight. Cook over charcoal.

# Steamed Fish

**Serves 2-3**

1 white meat fish such as mullet, cleaned and left whole
1 piece chung choi (preserved turnip), cut in tiny slivers
1 Tbsp. soy sauce
2 tsp. cornstarch
2 tsp. oil
1½ inch slice ginger, minced

2 Tbsp. white wine
1 tsp. salt
2 stalks green onion, minced

Combine all ingredients and rub over fish. Arrange in a dish, pouring any left over sauce over the fish. Steam for 15 minutes. Garnish with chopped Chinese parsley and serve immediately.

**Note:** If fish is too large to fit in a dish, cut in half.

# Oyster Sauce Beef
## & Chinese Peas

**Serves 4**

| | |
|---|---|
| 1½ lbs. beef (sirloin, flank) | ¼ c. oyster sauce |
| 1 Tbsp. cornstarch | 2 Tbsp. salad oil |
| 1 Tbsp. sugar | 2 cloves garlic, minced |
| 1 tsp. shoyu | ½ c. thinly sliced onion |
| 2 tsp. sherry | 1 c. Chinese peas |

Cut meat in thin strips. Combine all ingredients, except Chinese peas & onions. Heat oil and brown garlic; add meat mixture and onion. Stir fry 1 minute. Add peas and cook 1-2 minutes.

# Chicken and Peppers

**Serves 6**

4 whole chicken breasts, boned and cut in bite sized pieces

| | |
|---|---|
| ¼ c. soy sauce | 1-2 Tbsp. oil |
| 2 Tbsp. sherry | 2 medium green peppers, sliced |
| 1 Tbsp. cornstarch | dash of salt |
| 1 Tbsp. guava jelly | 3 stalks green onions |
| 1 tsp. minced ginger | walnuts or cashews for garnish |
| ½ tsp. crushed red pepper | |

Marinate chicken in soy sauce, sherry, cornstarch, jelly, ginger, and red pepper for 1 hour. Heat oil in a wok or skillet and stir fry the green peppers with salt until tender but crisp. Remove peppers from pan and stir fry the chicken. Return the peppers to the pan and add green onions. Garnish with pieces of walnut or cashews.

# Sweet Sour Tofu and Vegetables

**Serves 4**

1 block firm tofu
1 c. sliced pork or chicken
1 slice ginger root, crushed
1 c. chicken stock (or use 1 boullion cube dissolved in 1 c. water)
3 Tbsp. soy sauce
¼ c. vinegar
1 carrot, sliced
¼ c. Chinese peas
¼ c. water

2 Tbsp. oil
1 clove garlic, crushed

¼ c. sugar
3 bamboo shoots, sliced
1 small onion, sliced
2 tsp. cornstarch

Cut tofu into thick slices and drain. Heat oil in wok or skillet; saute pork or chicken with garlic and ginger. Add vinegar, stock, soy sauce, and sugar. Cook until meat is tender. Add tofu and vegetables and cook a few minutes. Thicken with cornstarch mixed with water.

# Jai
## Monk's Food

**Serves 4-6**

1 (5.5oz.) can water chestnuts
1 (5.5oz) can button mushrooms
1 c. dried chestnuts (shelled)
1 (5.5oz.) can bamboo shoots
4 pieces aburage (fried tofu)
2 (14.5oz) cans chicken broth
½ tsp. sugar

1 bundle long rice
1 (5.5oz) can ginko nuts
1 c. water
½ c. red bean curd
dash of soy sauce
1 tsp. salt
5 Tbsp. oil

Soak long rice in cold water for about 15 minutes. Remove from water and cut into 6 inch lengths. Soak dried chestnuts in hot water for about 45 minutes. Remove and set aside.

Heat oil in a large saucepan and saute water chestnuts, mushrooms, chestnuts, bamboo shoots, aburage, and ginko nuts for 3 minutes. Add chicken broth, water, bean curd, soy sauce, salt, and sugar. Bring to a boil and simmer for about 45 minutes.

**Note:** Other ingredients can be added or substituted. Dried red dates, lily flower, fungus, Chinese peas, fat choy (algae), and won bok are only some of the other ingredients that can be used.

# Eggplant with Hot Garlic Sauce

**Serves 3**

1 tsp. minced fresh red chili pepper or ¼ tsp. dried flakes
½ c. pork (or more), cut into strips

| | |
|---|---|
| 1 tsp. minced ginger | ½-¾ lb. eggplant |
| 1 tsp. minced garlic | 1½ Tbsp. soy sauce |
| 1 tsp. sugar | 1 tsp. white vinegar |
| 1 tsp. cornstarch | 1 c. oil |

In a small bowl mix together ginger, garlic, soy sauce, sugar, vinegar, chili pepper, & cornstarch. Set aside.

Heat oil in frying pan or wok until hot. Add eggplant, which has been peeled and sliced into 1 inch strips. Fry until pulp is brown but not burnt. Place between paper towels and lightly press down to extract excess oil. Add pork to pan and fry about 1 minute until pork is cooked. Remove pork and pour out oil. Heat sauce in pan until near boiling. Add pork and eggplant. Mix together until heated.

# Gau
## Chinese New Year's Pudding

**Makes 1 8-inch pan**

| | |
|---|---|
| 4¾ c. water (or more) | 3 Tbsp. oil |
| 3½ c. dark brown sugar | 1 red date |
| 2 lbs. mochi flour | sesame seeds |

Stir water and sugar together over low heat until sugar is dissolved. Bring to a boil, remove from heat and let cool. Add gradually to the flour and mix well. Add oil and mix well. Pour mixture into a pan or pyrex dish (about 8" in diameter and 3" deep) which has been lined with oiled ti leaves. Steam 3 hours.

1 c. fresh shredded coconut may be added to the pudding before steaming; mix well. When pudding is done, place 1 red date in the center and sprinkle with sesame seeds.

# Almond Float

**Serves 6**

1 envelope unflavored gelatin     1 c. evaporated milk
1 tsp. almond flavoring             3 Tbsp. sugar
1 c. boiling water                     ½ c. cold water
chilled fruit such as canned fruit cocktail, mandarin oranges,
    peaches, or lychee

Dissolve gelatin in one cup boiling water in a medium sized bowl. Add sugar and stir until dissolved. Add milk, cold water, and almond extract. Stir and pour into an 8 inch square pan. Refrigerate until set . . . at least 8 hours.

Place cubes of almond float in serving dishes. Spoon fruit and some of the syrup over the cubes.

# Japanese

**Introduction**

If one were asked what are the characteristics of a Japanese meal, the answers would be a pleasing appearance in the presentation of the food and a variety of dishes. Unlike American meals which are centered around one main dish, Japanese meals, like other Oriental meals, usually consist of several small dishes. But, no matter what the menu consists of, rice, *tsukemono* (pickled vegetables), and tea are considered necessities for any meal.

The Japanese consider it important to serve foods in a manner that is pleasing to the eye. They have a variety of small dishes and bowls to suit various foods. There are certain dishes in which to serve tsukemono and specific bowls for soup. It is considered uncouth to heap mounds of food on a plate or to heap a rice bowl.

The first Japanese immigrants came to the Hawaiian Islands around 1868 to work as laborers on the sugar plantations. With them they brought their food traditions. Basically, Japanese foods are simple and probably better for the health than the meat-heavy Western style meals. Today, in Hawai'i, Japanese families do not eat strictly Japanese foods. Western meals predominate among young families, while many of the typical Japanese foods remain a part of their menu. However, rice remains the staple starch.

There are a number of small Japanese delicatessens called *okazu-ya* in Hawai'i, and newcomers to the islands can sample a variety of everyday Japanese dishes at inexpensive prices. Traditional Japanese tea houses and Japanese restaurants are plentiful also, and here one can sample a more sophisticated type of Japanese meal served with the traditional manner and dinnerware. There are even special *sushi* bars for those who care to sample a variety of sushi.

### Cooking Methods

The Japanese home in Japan had no oven; therefore, cooking methods are confined to broiling or grilling over charcoal (*yakimono*), frying (*agemono*), steaming (*mushimono*), and simmering in a liquid (*nimono*). In addition, one-pot dishes which are not simmered (*nabemono*) are popular. *Sukiyaki* belongs to this classification of cooking.

Generally, Japanese food is cooked quickly; therefore, techniques of cutting were devised to allow food to cook evenly in a short period of time. These cutting methods not only expose greater surface area to the heat, but they present foods in a pleasing manner. *Rangiri,* a cutting technique applied to vege-

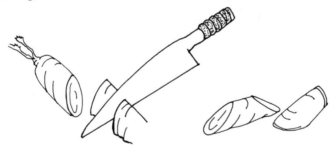

tables such as carrots, turnips, and bamboo shoots, means to cut on a diagonal, giving a half turn after each cut, then cutting on the opposite diagonal. This method is used in cutting vegetables for dishes such as *nishime. Sasagaki* means to cut into slivers.

The method is applied to root vegetables such as *gobo* (burdock) and is similar to sharpening a pencil with a knife. *Ichogiri* is a

method applied to cylindrical vegetables such as turnips and carrots. This method consists of thinly sliced crosswise pieces which are then quartered. Vegetables used in soups are often cut in this way.

Because Japanese do not use knives and forks, meats are generally cut up in bite-sized pieces also. Meat, chicken, and seafood are often skewered on bamboo skewers for grilling.

Japanese dishes are frequently cooked at the table. These dishes, familiar to most people, include sukiyaki, *shabu-shabu,* and *tempura.* Cooking at the table entails careful organization and preparation by the cook beforehand; however, the actual cooking time is short and presentation of the dish can be very impressive.

## Soybean and Bean Products

Traditional Japanese food includes the use of many soy-bean products. *Miso, tofu,* and *shoyu* (soy sauce) are all based on the soybean. The Buddhist background of the Japanese made them, in the early days, vegetarians who needed a source of high protein. Beef was introduced to Japan by the Portuguese traders during the 15th century, but beef has always been scarce and expensive in Japan. So, even today, soybean products play a large role in the Japanese diet.

Tofu (soybean curd), familiar to most island people, is sold locally in blocks submerged in water. It is very perishable and must be kept refrigerated. However, in recent years, a tofu which requires no refrigeration has been developed. Available in most large markets, this tofu is convenient because it can be kept on the shelf for many months. While tofu is bland in flavor, it is eaten uncooked and cold with soy sauce or is used cooked, in combination with other ingredients. It is a versatile ingredient for it can be fried, boiled, broiled, and used as a garnish as well. Tofu is high in protein, one 20 ounce block containing approximately 40 grams of protein.

There are also other Japanese ingredients derived from the plain tofu. The most well known of these derivatives is aburage, spongy, triangular or oblong pieces of deep fried tofu, which can be cut up and added to various dishes, or more often stuffed with sushi rice to form the popular inari sushi also known locally as cone sushi because of the triangular shape of the aburage.

The other tofu derivative which can be bought in most local supermarkets is called okara. This is the residue left behind after the soy milk has been pressed out of soybeans. It is sold in plastic bags, and in appearance it resembles shredded foam rubber. Seasoned with various vegetables and fish or shrimp, it makes a tasty addition to any Japanese meal. Containing half the protein and fat of tofu, okara's main contribution to the diet is fiber. It is also a very inexpensive source of protein.

Miso is another flavorful source of protein. It is a fermented soybean paste which is used basically as a seasoning. It has a high salt content and is a concentrated source of protein. Miso has similarities with yogurt because it contains many microorganisms and enzymes which aid in digestion. There are many varieties of miso, ranging in color from dark red to pale gold. Each has a distinct flavor. The most widely used miso in the islands is shiro or white miso, the pale colored, mild flavored variety.

Probably the most well known use of miso is in soup. Miso soup is part of the traditional Japanese breakfast and is thought to be an essential part of the diet for good health. It is popular with modern island Japanese families and is particularly nutritious when tofu and/or eggs are added to the soup.

Shoyu (soy sauce) is probably the key seasoning in Japanese cookery. It is used in place of salt, but because it is made from soybeans, it contains a trace of protein. In Japanese households, shoyu is kept in small bottles as table seasoning, along with the salt and pepper shaker. In Hawai'i, shoyu on the market shelves may be either island brewed or made in Japan. It is sold in bottles or large cans, ranging from 5 ounce table-sized bottles to one gallon cans. Many Japanese dishes start with a shoyu base, the most widely known dishes being sukiyaki and *teriyaki*.

Other bean and bean products in Japanese cooking include lima beans, black beans, and a red bean called *azuki*. Azuki, and sometimes lima beans, are most often used in sweetened and mashed form as a filling for *mochi* and *manju*, traditional Japanese sweets. Azuki beans are also combined with rice to make a celebration rice dish called *sekihan*. And black beans, cooked with sugar, is an important New Year's food.

**Vegetables**

The Japanese use an endless variety of vegetables. Like other Orientals, they rarely serve fresh, uncooked vegetables such as in a green salad. But green vegetables, Japanese style, are cooked very lightly, and their crispness and nutrients are retained. Japanese are also fond of pickled vegetables. Vegetables such as cucumbers, *daikon* (large white radishes), cabbage, mustard cabbage, and eggplant are pickled in salt and other seasonings. These pickles, called *koko* or *tsukemono*, are a necessity at a Japanese meal. In local markets, a great variety of ready-made tsukemono is available to the island shopper, but is is easy to make and many families prepare their own. One popular variety of tsukemono, called *takuwan*, is made out of daikon. It is said the takuwan is named after the Priest Takuan (1573-1645) who invented the method of preserving daikon. His method involved drying the radish in the sun then preserving in rice bran and salt with a heavy weight pressing on the vegetable. Today, simplified methods are used for making quick and easy

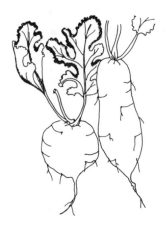

takuwan at home (see recipe section).

The Japanese salad is namasu, vegetables in a vinegar-sugar-salt sauce, sometimes with the addition of seaweed and seafood such as pieces of clam or slivers of raw fish. Namasu is most often made out of cucumbers, but radishes, turnips, and bean sprouts are also used.

Another vegetable dish which is used as a salad is aemono, lightly cooked vegetables mixed with a dressing. Dressings used include those made out of vinegar, miso, or tofu. A typical aemono dish is shira ae, vegetables combined with mashed tofu and miso.

## Fish and Seafood

The Japanese prefer fish and seafood to meat. Perhaps this stems from the fact that meat is not plentiful in Japan, but the Japanese really do like fish and seafood and they have an infinite number of ways to prepare them. Fish may be eaten raw as sashimi, used as a seasoning as flaked, dried bonito called katsuobushi, made into seasoned fishcake as in kamaboko, deep-fried to make shrimp or fish tempura, or used in soup bases called dashi.

Fish is always a part of a celebration meal, and it is one of the most widely used seasonings in Japanese food. Katsuobushi is one of the most valued seasonings in Japanese cookery. It is made from steamed then dried bonito which in its final form looks like a piece of hard wood. Flakes are scraped with a sharp knife or with a plane especially made for shaving katsuobushi. These flakes are packaged and sold in the Oriental food section of local supermarkets. Katsuobushi is used as a base for soup, sprinkled on boiled vegetables, or used as a seasoning for cooked vegetables.

Sashimi, raw slices of fish eaten with shoyu and mustard or horseradish, is very popular in the islands as well as in Japan. Prices of sashimi soar, particularly during the New Year's celebration; however, it is still widely consumed. While any fairly large fish can be used for sashimi, tuna (aku or skipjack; ahi or yellowfin) is the most widely used. The most important factor in its selection is freshness. Sashimi should be sliced fairly thin (¼" thick and 1½" wide) and arranged attractively on a platter with shredded raw vegetables as garnish.

Since ancient times in Japan, fish and sea products such as seaweed have been considered valuable gifts which connote joy and happiness. Katsuobushi implies victory (katsuo=victory; bushi=samurai), and therefore it is often presented as a gift of congratulation on happy occasions such as the birth of a child, a marriage, or any festivity. Large, whole red fish such as red snapper is a necessity at happy occasions too, for red is a happy color. Lobster, with its red, bent body symbolizes happiness and longevity.

**Meats**

Beef, pork, and chicken are used in Japanese dishes, but rarely does a Japanese dish consist mainly of a large piece of meat. The meat is generally thinly sliced and used in combination with vegetables and sauces. When meat is used alone, it is often cut up in small pieces and skewered on bamboo sticks before it is cooked. Probably the most widely known Japanese meat dish is sukiyaki. Either slices of beef or chicken may be used in this dish. Like most Japanese dishes, it combines many textures and varieties of vegetables with the meat and shoyu based sauce.

Another popular Japanese dish using meat is umani, also

known as nishime. Like sukiyaki, this dish is prepared in a shoyu based sauce. It uses either chicken or pork strips, but vegetables are the main ingredients. While sukiyaki must be eaten immediately to be at its best, nishime is more like a stew of meat and vegetables which are penetrated thoroughly with the cooking sauce. It is a dish that can be prepared in advance and eaten later at room temperature.

## Rice and Noodles

Rice is the staple starch among Japanese. While brown rice is known to be higher in nutritional value than white rice, Japanese in Japan as well as in Hawai'i prefer the white polished rice because traditionally, unhusked rice was considered a poor man's food. Steamed white rice is served at every Japanese home, and, in Hawai'i, it is the staple in homes of many non-Oriental families as well.

*Musubi* is known to almost all islanders. It is a way of making rice portable and easy to eat. Musubi is simply a rice ball. It may be plain rice, lightly salted or wrapped in black seaweed called *nori*. It sometimes has a sour preserved red plum tucked in its center. The sour plum keeps the rice from spoiling, and is a pleasant surprise as well. Musubi is taken on picnics and served for lunch, and is commonly sold at local Japanese delicatessens or *okazu-ya*.

*Sushi* refers to any vinegared rice. While in Hawai'i sushi usually brings to mind black rolls of seaweed wrapped rice (*maki sushi*) or "cones" or aburage filled with sushi rice (*inari sushi*), there are many other varieties of sushi, and sushi making is considered an art. *Nigiri sushi* are small oblongs of sushi rice

which are topped with a variety of tasty pieces of seasoned fish and seafood or vegetables. They are pretty to look at and are considered party food. Recently sushi bars have become popular in Hawai'i and in major cities throughout the United States. The popularity of sushi bars has made sushi a well known delicacy to mainland people.

Japanese are also fond of noodles. *Soba,* noodles made out of buckwheat, is a popular variety. It may be served hot or cold in a broth or with a shoyu based sauce, garnished with fishcake, meat, egg, shrimp, and vegetables. *Somen* and *udon* are two other varietes of noodles made out of wheat flour. Somen refers to thin noodles and udon refers to thick noodles. Both are usually served in broth with garnishes. Somen is frequently served cold, sometimes as a base for a salad. Like soba, somen is also served cold with merely a sprinkling of shoyu or *somen sauce,* which is available in the Oriental food section of local supermarkets. While most Americans eat noodles and soup quietly, the Japanese slurp their noodles as a sign of appreciation.

### Sweets

Because the Japanese did not have ovens, traditional Japanese sweets are usually steamed. Rice cakes called *mochi* play an important role in many traditional Japanese celebrations. *Manju,* another type of rice cake, is a small bun filled with sweetened bean paste (azuki or lima beans). They come in a variety of shapes, colors, and textures.

*Yokan* and *kanten* are two other Japanese desserts. Yokan is made out of bean paste and is a firm textured oblong which is cut into slices. Kanten, which has the same shape as yokan, is the Japanese version of gelatin. Made out of agar-agar (seaweed), it can be flavored in a variety of ways ranging from cinnamon to guava.

*Senbei* is another Japanese confection. These are sweet rice crackers which come in many shapes and sizes. They are light and crisp and are often served with tea as a snack. The Chinese fortune cookie, widely known to Americans, is a kind of senbei.

## Celebrations

The New Year, a most important event in Japanese life, is a time to bring good luck and prosperity to the home. Traditional New Year's foods have symbolic meanings, all of which have to do with good luck, good health, and happiness. In Hawai'i much of the symbolism has been lost or forgotten, but Japanese families continue to make and serve the traditional foods on New Year's day.

On New Year's eve, soba (buckwheat noodles) is traditionally served in a clear broth. Soba served on the eve is called *toshikoshi soba* (year crossing soba). It is said that long ago in Japan, goldsmiths and silversmiths used soba dough to collect scraps of gold and silver. Therefore, soba is associated with earning money and is eaten as a lucky charm ensuring a prosperous New Year. The noodles are also a symbol of longevity.

Mochi, steamed rice cake, is the most important New Year's food. Mochi is made by pounding hot mochi rice (glutinous rice) into a sticky dough which is then formed into various sized cakes. Mochi rice is a short grain rice that differs from conventional rice in its texture after it is cooked. It contains more dextrose than regular rice, some maltose, and no gluten, contrary to its name, glutinous rice. *Mochi-tsuki,* the rice pounding ceremony, takes place a few days before New Year's day. Men using large wooden mallets pound the mochi rice into the sticky dough in large wooden tubs. However, today most families buy commercially prepared mochi, sometimes even from the frozen food section of supermarkets.

Mochi has several symbolic meanings. In Japanese tradition it symbolizes longevity. Also, mochi, sounding like the Japanese word for wealthy (kane=root word for wealth; kane-mochi=rich person) symbolizes wealth and prosperity.

The traditional New Year's day breakfast for Japanese families consists of *ozoni,* a clear soup with mochi and vegetables in it. Ozoni may include in it *konbu* (seaweed), daikon (white radish), *mizuna* (a mild green vegetable), and sometimes cuttlefish. But, it always includes mochi. The ozoni is eaten to insure prosperity for the year.

Mochi is also placed on the household shinto altar as an offering at New Year's. Usually the mochi used for offering are larger in size than those used for eating, and two mochi are stacked on top of each other, an orange or tangerine topping the double mochi. In Japan dai-dai (a Japanese citrus fruit) is used instead of the orange or tangerine. Dai-Dai also means "generation after generation" in the Japanese language. While dai-dai is not available in the islands, the use of the orange fruit continues to symbolize the togetherness of the generations and a continuing life of prosperity. Other foods, such as seaweed and cuttlefish, along with traditional greenery (fern and pine) and pictures of good luck deities, complete the mochi altar offering which is known as kazali. In Hawai'i, while few people practice the shinto religion today, older Japanese continue to display the traditional kazali for luck.

Kuromame (black beans) is another important New Year's food. The black beans cooked in a sweet sauce with chestnuts (kuri) signifies good health because the word for bean, mămĕ is pronounced the same as "mame" which also means healthy.

Gobo (burdock) is often served at New Year's too. The burdock, a long, thin, brown root, goes deep into the soil. Gobo served on New Year's day serves as a symbol of deep family roots. It is most often served in unmani or nishime, a vegetable stew-like dish, or kimpira, a spicy dish seasoned with shoyu, sugar, and chili pepper.

Two kinds of seafood are served as part of the traditional New Year's meal. The first is tai (sea bream), a large red fish from Japan. Locally many people substitute other red-skinned fish

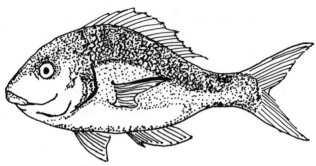

such as red snapper for tai. Tai is served at other happy occasions as well because the color red is considered lucky. Tai is also the ending of the word *medetai,* meaning happy. Medetai is also the root word for congratulations. The fish is always served whole with head and tail connected, signifying joy in wholeness.

The other symbolic seafood served at New Year's is *kazunoko* (herring roe), prepared in shoyu, often with the addition of *konbu* (seaweed). Eating kazunoko assures there will be many children for *kazu* means many; *ko* means children.

# Ozoni
## New Year's Soup

**Serves 6**

    1 lb. boned chicken, cut in bite sized pieces
    6 c. boiling water
    1 tsp. salt          1 tsp. shoyu
    2 dried mushrooms, soaked in water and then slivered
    ½ daikon (Japanese turnip), sliced diagonally
    ½ bunch mizuna (Japanese cabbage), blanched and cut in 1½
        inch pieces
    6 pieces mochi        kamaboko (fishcake), sliced thin

Simmer the chicken in water for 30 minutes. Add salt, shoyu, mushrooms, and daikon; simmer until diakon is tender. Boil mochi in water until soft and puffy. Arrange greens, mochi, and kamaboko slices in individual soup bowls and pour soup over all. Serve immediately.

# Cucumber Namasu
## Cucumber in Vinegar Sauce

**Serves 4**

2-3 cucumbers

¼ c. rice vinegar

1 tsp. ginger, minced

¼ c. sugar

¼ tsp. salt

To prepare cucumbers: Slice cucumbers in half; remove seeds if they are large. Slice in thin diagonal slices. Sprinkle with salt and let stand 20 minutes. Rinse, drain, and squeeze out excess water by putting cucumbers in a thin dish cloth or cheese cloth. Combine sugar, vinegar, salt, and ginger. Pour over cucumbers and chill.

**Variations:** Sliced carrots or celery may be added. Pieces of raw fish or boiled, canned shellfish such as slivered abalone or clams may also be added. Cleaned, blanched seaweed (ogo) may also be added.


# Gobo Kimpira
## Burdock Root in Sauce

**Serves 4-6** (side dish)

1½ fat gobo roots

1 Tbsp. sake

3 Tbsp. soy sauce

roasted sesame seeds

2 Tbsp. oil

1½ Tbsp. sugar

3 Tbsp. water

1 small red pepper, chopped fine

Scrape gobo; cut into shoe string slices about 1½ inches long. Soak in water with a little vinegar to prevent discoloring. Drain. In frying pan, saute the gobo in oil. Add all seasoning, except for sesame seeds. Cook until the liquid is gone. Put in a serving dish and sprinkle with roasted sesame seeds.

# Shira Ae
## Watercress - Tofu Salad

**Serves 4-6**

1 carrot, sliced in matchstick slivers and boiled
1 block konnyaku, cut in matchstick slivers
1 bunch watercress, cleaned and boiled
½ block tofu, boiled and squeezed

| | |
|---|---|
| 1 tsp. shoyu | 2 Tbsp. roasted sesame seeds |
| 3 Tbsp. miso | 2 Tbsp. sugar |

Bring watercress to a boil. Remove from heat, squeeze out water. Cut into 1 inch pieces. Boil carrot strips for a few minutes; squeeze out water. Place watercress and carrots in a bowl and sprinkle with shoyu. Put konnyaku in a pan and stir fry until it is dry. Crush sesame seeds with a mortar and pestle (suribachi). Boil tofu for about 5 minutes. Place in a cheesecloth or thin dish towel and squeeze out water. In a bowl, mix together tofu, ground sesame seeds, miso, and sugar. Add the konnyaku, watercress, and carrots. Mix well and chill.

# Takuwan
## Pickled Daikon

5-6 daikon (or turnips), peeled, sliced, placed in clean jars

Sauce:

| | |
|---|---|
| ¾ c. sugar | ¼ c. vinegar |
| 1 c. water | ¼ tsp. yellow food coloring |
| ¼ c. salt | 1 red chili pepper, chopped (optional) |

Boil all sauce ingredients together to dissolve the sugar. Cool. Pour over the sliced daikon. Place jars in the refrigerator. Ready to eat in 2 days.

# Basic Tempura Batter

½ c. flour

½ tsp. salt

1 egg

oil for frying

½ c. cornstarch

1 tsp. baking powder

½ c. cold water

2 drops yellow food coloring

Mix all ingredients together. Batter should be lumpy. Shrimp, deveined and flattened, sliced fish, vegetables such as slivered green beans and carrots, zucchini, eggplant, and sweet potato may be dipped in this basic batter and deep fried in vegetable oil over high heat. Drain on paper towels. Serve immediately with soy sauce or tempura sauce.

**Tempura Sauce:**

¼ c. soy sauce

½ c. water

¼ c. mirin (sweet rice wine)

3 Tbsp. katsuobushi (dry bonito flakes)

Bring all ingredients to a boil. Strain and serve as a dipping sauce.

# Sukiyaki

**Serves 4**

1 lb. tender beef such as sirloin, sliced as thin as possible

3 large dried mushrooms (or 1 small can sliced mushrooms)

1 bunch green onions

1 block firm tofu

½ c. soy sauce

½ c. sugar

1 bunch spinach

1 can shirataki (8 oz.)

1 can bamboo shoots (8 oz.)

½ c. mirin (sweet rice wine)

Wash the greens and chop them into 2-inch pieces. Cut the tofu into cubes. Drain bamboo shoots and slice diagonally. Drain the shirataki and cut in half. Remove stems from dried mushrooms and soak in warm water; when soft cut in bite-sized pieces. Arrange all ingredients including meat on a large platter. Using high heat, put soy sauce, mirin and sugar in a skillet. Bring to a boil to dissolve sugar. Cook the beef for a few minutes, then add the other ingredients. Add the greens last and serve with hot rice. Do not overcook.

**Note:** Chicken, boned and sliced thin can be substituted for the beef; other green vegetables such as Chinese cabbage (won bok)

or watercress may be substituted for spinach.

*Traditionally*, sukiyaki was cooked in front of the diners on a charcoal brazier. Today electric skillets are used. The ingredients should be arranged on the platter artfully so that the effect is pleasing to the eye.

# Nishime

**Serves 4-6**

1 lb. chicken breast, boned and sliced
1 c. carrots
1 c. bamboo shoots
3 dried mushrooms
½ c. water
¼ c. sugar
1 strip nishime konbu (seaweed)
1 c. gobo (burdock root)
5-6 Japanese taro (dasheen)
⅓ c. shoyu

Prepare vegetables: Soak konbu in water. When soft wash thoroughly and tie knots about 1½ inches apart. Cut konbu between the knots. Soak dried mushrooms in water until soft. Cut in pieces. Scrape gobo; cut in 1½ inch pieces. Soak in 1 c. water and 1 tsp. vinegar for 15 minutes. Peel Japanese taro and cut into chunks. Peel carrots and cut into diagonal pieces about ½ inch thick. Cut bamboo shoots into ½ inch slices also.

Brown chicken in small amount of vegetable oil. Add konbu, gobo, and water. Simmer 5 minutes. Add taro, carrots, bamboo shoots, and mushrooms. Cook until vegetables are done, about 5 minutes. Add shoyu and sugar. Toss and simmer a few minutes. Tastes better when made early in the day and vegetables are able to absorb the flavor of the sauce.

**Variations:** Pork may be used in place of chicken. Other vegetables such as turnips, Chinese peas, or konnyaku may be added or substituted.

# Yaki Tori Kushi
### Chicken on a Stick

Boned chicken breasts or thighs, cut in bite sized pieces
Fresh mushrooms
skewers
Green peppers, cut in cubes

**Sauce:**

½ c. shoyu

½ c. sake

2 Tbsp. miso

1 tsp. grated ginger

1 c. mirin (sweet rice wine)

3 Tbsp. sugar

red pepper flakes (optional)

Cook sauce ingredients in a large pan over low heat for ½ to 1 hour. If using bamboo skewers, soak skewers in water, so they will not burn. Alternate chicken, green peppers, and mushrooms on skewers. Grill or broil chicken, brushing sauce on the skewers at least 3 times. Serve with hot rice.

Any left over sauce may be refrigerated and used again. It will keep 3-4 months.

# Sushi

**Basic Sushi Rice:** All types of sushi can be made from this rice.

Wash 3 c. calrose rice. Add 3 c. water and cook in rice cooker. To cook on stove, bring rice to boil in a covered saucepan. Simmer for 15 minutes. Remove pan from stove and let sit for another 10-15 minutes. **makes 9 cups**

*Vinegar Sauce*

½ c. Japanese rice vinegar

½ c. sugar

1 tsp. salt

Cook over medium heat until sugar dissolves. Cool. Place cooked rice in a large mixing bowl. Sprinkle half of vinegar sauce over the hot rice; mix gently. Taste. Add more vinegar sauce if desired.

**I. Nigiri Sushi** (Finger Sushi)

*Toppings:*

sashimi (raw fish), cooked shrimp, cooked octopus, caviar, sliced cucumber, takuwan, etc.

*Mustard Paste:*

Make a paste out of 4 tsp. dry mustard, 2 tsp. of water, and 1 tsp. shoyu.

Shape sushi rice into oblongs about 1" x 2½"; flatten slightly. Pat mustard paste on rice; press desired topping on top. Dip in shoyu to eat.

## II. Inari Sushi (Cone Sushi)                                    **16 cones**

*To Prepare sushi cones:*

*8 aburage (fried bean curd) and 2 c. water*

Cut aburage in half to form cones. Take out inner part carefully and reserve for vegetable sauce. Cook aburage cones in water for 30 minutes. Drain; squeeze out excess liquid.

*Seasoning for cones:*

*1½ c. broth (use packaged Japanese broth such as Dashi No Moto)*

*1 Tbsp. shoyu*               *2 Tbsp. fish flakes or dried shrimp*

*½ tsp. salt*                 *3 Tbsp. sugar*

Combine all ingredients in a pan and simmer the aburage in it for 15-20 minutes. Drain and squeeze gently. Fill with vegetable-sushi rice.

*Vegetables for rice:*

*3 dried mushrooms, softened in water then minced*

*1 Tbsp. dry fish flakes or dry shrimp*

*½ c. minced carrot*          *½ c. minced green beans*

*½ tsp. salt*                 *inner part of aburage, minced fine*

*1 Tbsp. sugar*              *¼ c. shoyu*

*1 c. water*

Cook all ingredients together for 10 minutes or until carrots are tender. Drain and add to the basic sushi rice. Loosely pack the rice into the cones.

## III. Maki Sushi (rolled sushi)

*9 c. sushi rice and 10 sheets sushi nori (seaweed)*

*Filling:*

*1 2oz. pkg. kampyo (dried gourd)*

*1 carrot, cut lengthwise in ½ inch strips*

*10 pieces of watercress, blanched*

*8-10 dried mushrooms, softened in water and cut in thin strips*

*1 3½oz. can unagi (seasoned eel) or kamaboko (fishcake) cut in strips*

*Preparation:*

*Kampyo:* Soak in water 15 minutes, rinse and drain. Mix 2 Tbsp. soy sauce with 1 Tbsp. sugar. Bring to boil in small pan, add kampyo. Simmer 2 minutes. Cool and cut in 10 inch lengths.

*Mushrooms and Carrots:* Cook carrots until tender, but not

mushy. Mix 2 Tbsp. soy sauce, 1 Tbsp. sugar, and 1 Tbsp. water in small pan. Cook carrots and mushrooms in this sauce 5 minutes. Cool.

Assembling the rolls:

Place nori on sudare (bamboo mat) with edge closest to you ½ inch from edge of the sudare.

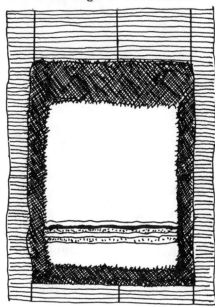

Spread sushi rice over nori, about ½ inch thick, leaving about a 1½ inch margin on edge farthest from you. Arrange filling ingredients 1 inch from the edge closest to you— 5 strands kampyo, 1 row each of mushrooms, carrot, watercress, eel. Roll away from your body as you would a jelly roll. Work slowly, pressing with the hands to keep ingredients in place. Cut each roll into 8 pieces using a wet knife.

# Custard Mochi

½ c. butter or margarine
2 c. sugar
4 eggs
2 tsp. vanilla

4 c. milk
3 tsp. baking powder
2 c. mochiko (glutinous rice flour)

Grease and flour a 9 x 13 inch pan. Cream butter and sugar. Add eggs and beat well. Add mochiko and baking powder with 2 cups of milk. Mix well, then add the remaining milk. Bake at 350 degrees for 1 hour. Cool completely before cutting. Keep refrigerated.

Note: This is not a true mochi, but has the texture and flavor of mochi.

# Portuguese

## Introduction

The first Portuguese came to Hawai'i in 1878 to work as plantation laborers. Most of the Portuguese who came to Hawai'i came not from Portugal itself, but from the islands of Madeira and the Azores which are located to the west of Portugal. Among the first Europeans to come to Hawai'i, they brought with them European-style foods and baked goods which contrasted greatly with the foods brought by the Oriental immigrants.

Portuguese food can be characterized as plain and hearty food of the common people. Wholesome, nutritious soups and casseroles are typical. Spices, herbs, red pepper, vinegar, and garlic are widely used to create unusual flavor combinations in common foods. Egg-rich breads and pastries are a Portuguese favorite, and today Portuguese sweet bread or *pao doce* and doughnuts called *malassadas* are very much a part of Hawai'i's food legacy. Hot and spicy Portuguese sausage or *linguica*, blood sausage, and spicy pickled onions are all available in local supermarkets. For breakfast, Portuguese sausage, eggs, and rice are as common in Hawai'i as bacon, eggs, and toast are elsewhere.

While there are only a few restaurants in Hawai'i specializing in a wide variety of Portuguese dishes, Portuguese bean soup and Portuguese sausage are available on the menus of many restaurants. But because Portuguese food contains ingredients that are basic and familiar to most people, it is not difficult to prepare in one's own home.

Some popular traditional Portuguese foods include Portu-

60

guese bean soup, *caldo verde* (cabbage soup with beans or potatoes), *carne vinha d'alhos* (marinated meat), and *bacalhau* (codfish).

Portuguese cookery encompasses all cooking methods from roasting to frying to slow simmering. A European people, they are generally credited with introducing the oven and baked goods to the islands.

## Meats

Pork is a favorite meat in Portuguese cookery, although beef, lamb, and all types of poultry are used as well. Vinegar and spices are frequently used in the preparation of meat dishes. No doubt this stems from the fact that years ago in Portugal, meats were preserved in brine. Today, carne vinha d'alhos, meat marinated in wine, vinegar, garlic, and spices is still a favorite way of preparing meat. *Vinha* means wine; *alhos* means garlic. Fish as well as poultry and the traditional pork or beef may be prepared using this method.

Probably the most well known type of Portuguese meat is the Portuguese sausage known as linguica. Made from pork, linguica has a very distinctive flavor which makes it different

from other sausages. Its flavoring comes from vinegar, spices, garlic, and red pepper. There are many different brands available locally with flavors ranging from mild to hot and spicy. Linguica is most frequently fried, but it is also used in combination with other ingredients in soups and casseroles.

*Chorizo* is another type of Portuguese sausage. The principal difference between linguica and chorizo is that of seasoning. Chorizo is usually spicier and hotter than the linguica. Linguica, the more popular of the two, may be substituted in any recipe calling for chorizo. *Morcela,* or blood sausage, is still another kind of sausage enjoyed by the Portuguese.

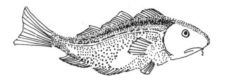

## Fish and Seafood

The Portuguese come from a seafaring country and seafood has traditionally been an important part of their diet. Coming to Hawai'i they were able to assimilate local fish into their diet. However, codfish (bacalhau), not a local fish but a staple in Portugal, remained a favorite with the Portuguese. Bacalhau is salted, dried codfish and it usually takes some preparation before actual cooking. The codfish is soaked overnight in cold water. Then it is drained and rinsed again before being cooked in combination with other ingredients. There are many traditional Portuguese dishes that use this fish.

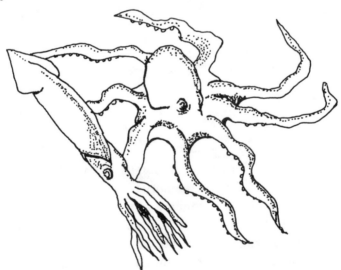

Octopus, squid, and shellfish are also enjoyed by the Portuguese. Again, they tend to prepare octopus and squid by cooking them in wine and vinegar or by pickling. Sometimes they are combined with vegetables and spices and herbs to make a stew or casserole.

## Vegetables

Green vegetables are used in Portuguese cookery as well as fresh in salads. Cabbage, watercress, and kale (also known as Portuguese cabbage) are favorite green vegetables. Peas, green beans, turnips, tomatoes, and onions are also well used. Garlic is used heavily as a seasoning.

Vegetables appear in soups and casseroles and they are also marinated in vinegar and oil. One popular side dish is pickled onions.

## Sweets

The Portuguese have many desserts and sweets. *Pudim flan* is a traditional custard dessert that is rich with eggs and milk. It may be served plain or with various sauces. Baked goods such as sponge cake, honey cake, and filled pastries are also favorites. During the Easter season and Christmas, traditional baked goods are served. These include *massa sovada* or Easter bread, malassadas, *bulo de mel* or honey cakes, and *braoas,* which are similar to sugar cookies.

## Starches

The Portuguese have a rather starchy diet. Beans, rice, potatoes, macaroni, and bread are all part of the diet and often more than one starch is served at a meal. While the Oriental immigrants brought rice as their staple to the islands, the Portuguese brought bread. Their original crisp crust white bread

was baked in outdoor ovens called *fornos tejollos* (stone ovens), or more commonly, *fornos*. Portuguese families built the forno in their back yards. They were igloo-shaped and approximately six feet high and five and a half feet in diameter. Fornos were constructed out of cement, bricks, and stone with walls at least six inches thick. Wood was used to fuel the oven. The typical forno held an average of twelve loaves of bread which were put in and taken out with a long handled wooden spade. Fornos are no longer used today, but the Portuguese are still fond of good bread.

Pao doce, sweet bread, was also baked in the forno. Originally, this egg-rich bread was reserved for special holidays. Today, the popular bread is available at most local bakeries and markets and even at the airport for visitors to take home as a special treat from Hawai'i.

Bread is also used in combination with other ingredients. One unique Portuguese dish called *acorda* is a bread soup. Acorda is prepared with fish, chicken, or seafood along with vegetables, garlic, oil, and always bread. Eggs are often poached in the hot broth of acorda.

Beans are an important source of protein and carbohydrate in the Portuguese diet. White beans, red beans, and lima beans are often used. They are made into soups and added to casserole

dishes. Portuguese bean soup is probably the most well known Portuguese dish. There is no such thing as one "Portuguese soup." There are many ways of preparing this hearty soup; each is highly individual. Some recipes use red beans such as kidney beans or pinto beans while others use small white beans such as navy beans. Toasted beans, chick peas, corn and *tremocos* (lupine seeds) are enjoyed as snack food.

Potatoes and yams are also part of the Portuguese diet. Potatoes are fried, boiled, and used in soups and casseroles. Like other island people, the Portuguese include rice as a staple. It is usually served plain, but is sometimes cooked in combination with other foods.

## Celebrations

Because the Portuguese are Catholics, most of their festive occasions are connected with religious holidays, Easter and Christmas being the most important. Birthdays, baptisms, and weddings are also widely celebrated.

Ash Wednesday, the first day of Lent, is the beginning of a time of abstinence from meat and meat products for the Catholic Portuguese. Malassadas, which were originally cooked in lard, an animal fat, would be one of the foods refrained from during the Lenten season. So Malassadas Day, the Tuesday before Ash Wednesday, was created by someone. The thought behind this day was to have one last fling with food cooked in animal fat before settling down to the religious discipline dictated by Lent. Malassadas Day is observed by the Portuguese who live in the Azores and Madeira where the Hawai'i Portuguese came from. On this day large quantities of malassadas are made and distributed to friends and family. It is unique because it survives as a tradition for Hawai'i's Portuguese, but is not observed by Portuguese living elsewhere in the United States or even in Portugal itself.

Also during the Easter season, a traditional bread called massa sovada is baked. This sweet bread is baked with a whole

egg (in its shell) on top. It is said that the egg symbolizes the joy of the Easter season, or fertility, or the resurrection of Christ. Often more than one egg, sometimes tinted with Easter egg dye, is put on top of a loaf of bread.

The Holy Ghost Festival (*Festa do Espirito Santo*) is one of the important occasions in the local Portuguese community. The origin of the festival has been traced to Queen Isabel of Aragon who lived in 14th century Portugal. She was known as a charitable and religious woman who built a church dedicated to the Holy Ghost. She also founded a cult known as "The Coronation of the Emperor" from which the present day Holy Ghost Festival grew.

In the original ceremony a man who represented the emperor goes to the church of Sao Francisco on Easter accompanied by nobility and commoners. With him are two men in the role of kings, and three pages, each carrying a crown. They offer the crowns to God and a priest crowns the emperor and kings. They then join a festive procession which honors Christ the resurrected. Later in the day the emperor leaves the Holy Ghost Church carrying the Queen's crown and goes to the convent of Sao Francisco to be crowned again. There is festivity and dancing and the emperor again offers his crown to the altar, but is again presented with it by the priest. He then sits on a throne and is treated like a real king. The same action is re-enacted on each of the following Sundays until the Day of the Holy Ghost. On the final day of the festival the priest blesses the bread and meat which are distributed to the poor at the Holy Ghost Church.

In Hawai'i, as in other American Portuguese communities, Holy Ghost Societies still exist, although the original coronation of the emperor has been replaced by the coronation of a queen of the festival. While the festival varies from group to group, generally it follows a traditional pattern. The festival lasts for seven weeks, beginning the first Saturday after Easter. In one Holy Ghost Society, members place names of their children in a vase and seven names are drawn. The families of each of the children whose names are drawn are responsible for a week of the Holy Ghost Festival. During each of the weeks the family of that child is responsible for social activities and refreshments for the group. The person whose name is drawn for the seventh week chooses the queen of the celebration. The queen may be anyone that person chooses.

The finale of the local Holy Ghost Festival is marked by a kind of fair. Non-traditional foods such as stew and hot dogs are sold as well as the traditional foods, malassadas and lupine beans. Also during the finale, bread and meat are blessed by the priest. Whereas this blessed bread and meat was originally distributed to the poor, it is now purchased with society dues and given to the members. The culmination of the festival is marked by the coronation of the queen. A procession goes from the Holy Ghost Society to the Catholic church where mass and festivities follow. While the original ceremony is only loosely followed today, it does help to preserve some of the tradition.

In some Portuguese homes the tradition of the *lapinha* is observed at Christmas. The lapinha, a nativity scene built in tiers, displays the creche in the center. Arrangements of figurines, rock, greenery, and food offerings such as fruit and nuts are placed around the scene. Seven days before Christmas small white bowls of wheat seeds called *trigo* are started. Water is poured over the seeds and they are allowed to sprout. By Christmas Eve the wheat reaches appropriate height to be placed on the lapinha. If the wheat grows green and tall it is said that good fortune will come to the family; if the wheat dies prematurely,

bad luck will supposedly prevail. On Christmas Eve candles are lit and the baby Jesus is placed on the top tier of the lapinha at midnight. Traditionally, carolers serenaded the lapinha and were later served sweets such as *rosquilhas* (ring-shaped cakes) and braoas (round cakes similar to sugar cookies). On the sixth of January, the Feast of the Three Kings (marking the arrival of the Three Kings in Bethlehem), the lapinha is taken down and the wheat planted. This marks the conclusion of the Christmas season and the beginning of new life.

# Sabula de Vinha
### Pickled Onions

Take small white or Maui onions (enough to fill a quart jar), cut in half or quarters, and place in jar.

Add:

1 clove garlic, crushed
2 chili peppers, seeds re-
    moved and crushed
Cider vinegar (to fill ⅔ of jar)
Water (to fill remaining ⅓ of jar)

1 Tbsp. Hawaiian salt
1 tsp. sugar

Cover jar tightly; shake well and let stand 2 - 3 days, shaking jar at least once a day. Refrigerate.

# Caldo Verde
### Kale Soup

**Serves 6**

1 lb. kale or greens such as broccoli, mustard greens, or
    collard greens
¾ lb. beef (chuck) cut into ¾ inch cubes
10 oz. mild linguica, cut into ½ inch slices
⅓ lb. dried white beans          6 Tbsp. olive oil
8 c. boiling water               3 onions, cut into thin wedges
salt and pepper to taste

Soak the beans in water overnight. Rinse and drain. Heat oil in a large pot and add onions. Cook until the onions are golden. Add half the boiling water and salt to taste. Bring to a boil and add beef, linguica, and beans. Simmer 1 hour, skimming the surface to remove scum.

Remove tough stems from greens and shred finely. Add remaining boiling water and the greens to the pot and simmer for 1½ hours. Add more salt and pepper to taste.

# Soupa de Feijaos
## Portuguese Bean Soup

**Serves 6 - 8**

½ lb. kidney or small red beans (soaked in water overnight)
1 Portuguese sausage (about 10oz.), sliced, fried, and drained

| | |
|---|---|
| 2 ham hocks | 1 clove garlic |
| Water | 1 large onion, chopped |
| 1 potato, diced | 2 stalks celery, diced |
| 3 carrots, sliced | 1 8oz. can tomato sauce |

4 c. cabbage, coarsely chopped
watercress, cut in 1 inch pieces (optional)

Drain beans; place in a Dutch oven or soup pot. To the beans add ham hocks and garlic. Cover with water. Simmer 3 hours or until meat and beans are tender. Remove ham hocks and discard bones and fat; cut ham into bite sized pieces. Add onion, celery, carrots, tomato sauce, ham and cooked sausage to the soup and cook until carrots are almost tender. Add potato and cook until soft. Add cabbage and cook until it is tender. Garnish with chopped watercress just before serving.

**Variations:** This is a basic recipe. Other vegetables of your choice may be added. Some people also add about ½ c. of macaroni.

# Portuguese Pickled Fish

**Serves serves 6**

1 lbs. cod or other firm fleshed white fish

| | |
|---|---|
| 1½ c. wine vinegar | ½ tsp. thyme |
| 3 cloves garlic, crushed | 1 red chili pepper |
| 2 tsp. salt | ¼ c. olive oil |
| 6 whole cloves | 2 bay leaves |

Cut fish into serving sized pieces. Combine all ingredients except olive oil and marinate the fish overnight. Cook fish in sauce for 10 minutes. Drain the fish and fry it in hot oil until it is browned.

# Bacalhau
## Codfish Cakes

**Serves 3 - 6**

1 lb. salted codfish
¾ c. olive oil
1 onion, chopped
½ tsp. mint, chopped
½ tsp. salt
½ tsp. black pepper

2 c. coarsely crumbled day old bread
¼ c. coriander, chopped
1 Tbsp. parsley, chopped
3 cloves garlic, crushed
2 tsp. paprika
1 small chili pepper, minced (opt.)

Place cod in a glass or stainless steel bowl or pan. Cover with cold water and soak at least 12 hours, changing water 2-3 times. Drain the cod, rinse, and place in a saucepan. Cover with water and bring to a boil. (Taste water at this point; if it seems too salty, drain the water and repeat process). Reduce heat to low and simmer, uncovered, until fish flakes easily (about 20 minutes).

Drain. When it is cool enough to handle, remove and discard skin and bones. Shred the fish finely with fingers.

In a large bowl combine bread and ½ c. of the olive oil. Beat and mash them together until oil is absorbed. Add coriander, parsley, onions, mint, paprika, salt, pepper, chili pepper, and bread to the flaked cod. Beat with a spoon until the ingredients are combined. Shape the mixture into 6 flat round patties, about ½ inch thick and 3½ inches in diameter.

In a heavy skillet, heat the remaining ¼ c. of oil and add the garlic. Cook for 2-3 minutes; remove and discard garlic. Cook the codfish cakes in the hot oil for about 3 minutes on each side or until golden brown. Garnish with parsley. Traditionally, these cakes are topped with a freshly poached egg before serving.

# Carne de Vinha D'Alhos
## Pickled Pork

**Serves 8**

4 lbs. pork butt
1 c. water
5 bay leaves
6 whole cloves
1½ tsp. salt

1 c. wine vinegar
½ c. dry white wine
6 cloves garlic, crushed
3 red chili peppers
½ tsp. pepper

Cut pork into small pieces (about 2 inches). Combine all ingredients in a large glass bowl and add pork. Cover and refrigerate for 2 days, turning the meat daily to permit seasoning to penetrate all pieces.

Cook the pork in this liquid, stirring off and on until meat is brown. Or, drain off the liquid and fry pork in an ungreased pan on low heat until meat is brown and cooked through.


# Caldeirada
## Seafood Stew

**Serves 8**

1 onion, chopped
1 green pepper, chopped
1 20 oz. can of tomatoes
½ tsp. pepper
3 cloves garlic, minced
½ tsp. salt
⅔ c. olive oil
24 small clams, washed
  and scrubbed

1½ lbs. each of 2 kinds of firm white fish such as bass, snapper, mahimahi, or cod
1½ lbs. squid, cleaned and cut into 2 inch strips
1 c. dry white wine
8 thick slices white bread, cut into triangles

Combine onion, green pepper, tomatoes, garlic, pepper, and salt in a bowl and mix thoroughly.

Place clams in a large casserole or Dutch oven and pour in ⅓ c. of the olive oil. Place half of the vegetable mixture over the clams and add the fish and squid. Spread rest of vegetable mixture on top and pour in the wine. Bring to a boil and reduce heat to low. Cover and simmer undisturbed for 20 minutes, or until clams open and fish flakes easily.

Heat the remaining ⅓ c. oil in a skillet. Add the bread and brown well on both sides. Drain on paper towels. To serve place two triangles of bread in each soup plate and ladle the soup over the bread. Arrange clams, fish and squid on top and garnish with parsley.

# Broa
## Portuguese Cornbread

**Makes 1 loaf**

| | |
|---|---|
| 1 pkg. dry yeast | 1½ c. white or yellow cornmeal |
| 1½ tsp. salt | 1 tsp. sugar |
| 1 c. boiling water | ¼ c. lukewarm water |
| 4 tsp. olive oil | 1½-2 c. flour |

Pulverize the cornmeal in a blender or food processor. Combine 1 c. cornmeal, salt, and boiling water; mix until smooth. Stir in 3 tsp. olive oil and allow mixture to cool. Dissolve yeast and sugar in lukewarm water. Set aside until yeast doubles in volume. Stir yeast into cornmeal mixture. Gradually add the remaining cornmeal and 1 c. of the flour, stirring well.

Form dough into a ball and place in a greased bowl. Cover with a dish towel and set dough in a warm place until double in bulk. Coat a 9 inch round pan with the remaining olive oil. Turn dough onto a floured board and knead for 5 minutes, adding as much of the flour as you can until dough is firm but not stiff. Shape into a round, flat, loaf. Place in the pan and cover with a towel. Let rise until double in bulk. Bake in 350 degree oven for 40 minutes or until golden.

Serve with bean soup or caldo verde.

# Massa Sovada
### Easter Bread

**Makes 2, 9-inch loaves**

2 pkgs. dry yeast
1 c. milk, scalded
¼ c. warm water
3 eggs, well beaten
1 c. sugar

½ c. butter, melted
1 tsp. lemon extract
6 c. flour (approximately)
1 tsp. salt
6 raw eggs in shells, tinted

Scald milk. Dissolve yeast in warm water. Beat eggs; add dissolved yeast to them. Add sugar, melted butter, and lemon extract. Gradually stir in flour and salt. Turn dough out on a floured board and knead until it is smooth (about 20 minutes). Place in a large greased bowl, grease the top, cover and let rise until double in bulk (about 2-3 hours).

Punch down the dough and divide into 2 loaves. Place each in a buttered 9 inch pie or cake pan. Cover and let rise again.

When the loaves are double in bulk, carefully scoop out 3 egg shaped amounts of dough from the top of each loaf. Into the hollows carefully place the eggs. Roll the removed dough and place strips of it over each egg to form crosses. Brush tops of the loaves with milk and bake in a 350 degree oven for 40 minutes or until golden brown.

# Malassadas
### Sweet Doughnuts

**Makes 24**

½ c. milk
1¼ c. sugar
½ tsp. salt
3 eggs
sugar for rolling

1 cake compressed yeast or dry yeast
2 Tbsp. lukewarm water
¼ c. butter, melted
2¾ c. flour
1 qt. salad oil for frying

Heat milk to lukewarm. Moisten yeast in lukewarm water. Add the yeast, salt, sugar, and melted butter to the milk. Stir in part of the flour, beating well with a wooden spoon to prevent lumps. Add beaten eggs and remaining flour to form a soft dough. Cover the dough and set it in a warm place until it doubles in bulk.

Heat oil to 350 degrees. Drop dough by tablespoonful into the hot oil and fry until evenly browned. Drain on absorbent paper and roll in sugar.

# Arroz Doce
Sweet Rice

**Serves 4**

| | |
|---|---|
| 1½ c. milk | 6 pieces lemon peel, about 1½" x ½" |
| 6 c. water | ½ c. rice (not instant) |
| 1 tsp. vanilla | 3 egg yolks |
| ½ tsp. cinnamon | ⅓ c. sugar |
| salt | |

In a saucepan, bring milk, vanilla, cinnamon, lemon peel, and a dash of salt to a boil. Cover the pan, remove from heat, and let stand 30 minutes.

Boil water. Pour in the rice in a steady stream, allowing the water to boil continuously. Add ¼ tsp. salt, reduce heat to low and continue to boil rice uncovered for 15-20 minutes. Drain in a colander then spread rice out on layers of paper towels.

In a bowl beat egg yolks and sugar together with an electric mixer until they are light and lemon colored. Beating constantly, pour milk in a thin, steady steam. Return the mixture to saucepan and cook over low heat, stirring constantly until custard thickens enough to coat the spoon lightly. Add rice and continue to cook for 3 minutes, stirring constantly. Pour pudding into a dish about 12 inches x 8 inches and no more than ½ inch deep. Cool to room temperature. Just before serving, sprinkle with cinnamon.

# Puerto Rican

## Introduction

The first Puerto Ricans arrived in Hawai'i in 1900. Recruited to work on sugar plantations by the Hawai'i Sugar Planter's Association, they left one island home to come to another. Puerto Ricans have their roots in three ethnic groups: the Indians who were the original inhabitants of the island, the Spanish who colonized it in 1493, and the Africans who were brought to work on plantations as slaves. Today pure blooded Puerto Ricans are not a major ethnic group in Hawai'i, numbering approximately 4,000. But they were one of the original island immigrant groups and it is estimated that about 20,000 people in Hawai'i are of part Puerto Rican ancestry.

Puerto Rican food and customs are Spanish in tradition. The food is best described as hearty and mildly spicy. Thick, heavy soups and stews, casseroles of rice, beans, and meat, and turnovers with meat stuffings are typical. The seasoning of the food is typically Spanish. Coming from one tropical environment to another similar environment, Puerto Ricans found that some of their basic foods already existed in Hawai'i. Fruits familiar to them such as papayas, mangoes, and bananas flourished, and crops such as yams, *yautia* (a type of taro), and *gandul* (pigeon peas) were easily cultivated.

Puerto Rican food can be easily prepared at home because most of the ingredients are readily available in supermarkets, although a few items such as *achiote* seeds (of the annato or lipstick tree) which give Puerto Rican dishes their characteristic orange color, and plantains, green starch bananas, are available only in special grocery stores.

## Cooking Methods

$F$rying, stewing, and baking are the principal cooking methods used to prepare Puerto Rican food. Puerto Ricans are especially fond of fried turnovers (*pastelillos*) and fritters. Traditionally, lard was used for frying, but today vegetable oil has replaced lard.

Many Puerto Rican dishes are slow cooked or stewed. Hearty soups and meat and vegetable stews are traditional foods. Unlike the Orientals, Puerto Ricans have baked foods. Main dishes are baked as well as custards, cakes, and cookies for desserts.

No special utensils are necessary for Puerto Rican cookery. A mortar and pestle makes grinding spices and herbs easier. And a grater or food processor makes preparation of coconut and grated plantains easier.

## Seasonings

$B$asic seasonings for Puerto Rican dishes are spices such as oregano, cayenne pepper, ginger, garlic, pimento, and coriander or cilantro (Chinese parsley). Many of the foods have an orange color which is achieved by the use of achiote seeds. These seeds, also known as *annato*, are small red seeds which are simmered in vegetable oil or lard until the fat is tinged with color. No distinct flavor comes from the seeds; they are used mainly to achieve a reddish orange color. The fat is strained, then stored in jars in the refrigerator. Some cooks use tomato paste rather than achiote fat to achieve the desired color in foods.

Another ingredient basic to Puerto Rican cookery is *sofrito*. This is a tomato sauce that is a blend of salt pork, ham, tomatoes, green peppers, garlic, and spices. Sofrito serves as a basic sauce for cooking stews and casseroles; it is kept in the refrigerator and used as needed.

## Meats, Fish, Poultry

Beef, pork, and poultry are all used in Puerto Rican cookery, although pork is one of the favorite meats. It is used in several dishes in combination with vegetables, beans, or rice. Ham is often cut up and added to dishes for flavor, and pork rind is enjoyed as a snack called *chicharrones* (cracklings). *Lechon asado* (roast suckling pig), is often prepared for holiday feasts and is considered a delicacy.

Chicken is used in many dishes. It is often cooked together with rice and vegetables. *Arroz con pollo* (chicken and rice) and *chicken asopao* (a glorified chicken and rice) can be called the Puerto Ricans' national dishes.

All kinds of fresh fish and seafood are used. The Spanish influence can be seen again in the use of salted codfish. There are numerous recipes utilizing this fish known as *bacalao*. It is used in everything from salad to stew.

Often more than one variety of meat is used in one dish. *Sancocho* (vegetable stew) for example, uses beef, pork and ham, and *paella* uses chicken, pork, and shellfish.

In addition to meats and fish, eggs serve as another source of protein. They are used frequently in omelets and in egg rich puddings and custards. Eggs are also used to bake cakes such as pound cake and sponge cake.

## Vegetables

Besides using starchy vegetables previously mentioned, Puerto Ricans use other vegetables in their cooking. They are used in casseroles and stews, stuffed with meats and cheese, or boiled or fried and served as an accompaniment to other foods.

Green peppers, tomatoes, and onions are probably the most widely used vegetables. They are necessary ingredients in sofrito and flavor many other dishes. *Chayote,* a kind of green squash, and pumpkin are often used, as are eggplant and okra. Watercress,

swiss chard, and lettuce are used to a lesser degree. Generally it can be said that Puerto Rican cooks tend to use more starchy tubers or root vegetables rather than leafy green vegetables.

## Starches

Rice is the staple starch of the Puerto Rican diet, having been brought to the islands by Columbus. Rice is cooked in combination with meat, poultry, or beans. It is also eaten plain and used in desserts.

Beans are also a source of carbohydrate and protein for the Puerto Ricans. Kidney beans, chick peas (garbanzo beans), cowpeas, and pigeon peas (gandul) are used in various dishes. Pigeon peas are not familiar to most people. They are a tropical legume

which probably made their way to Puerto Rico through African slaves. Easily cultivated in Hawai'i's climate, these reddish beans are a good source of protein, as are other beans. Many Puerto Rican dishes combine beans and rice to make a complete protein meal using very little meat.

Another source of carbohydrate in the Puerto Rican diet comes from plantains or cooking bananas. Plantains are meaty bananas with a high starch content and lower sugar content than regular eating bananas. They are picked green and the flesh is grated to make a "dough" in which a spicy pork mixture is wrapped to make *pastele,* a well known Puerto Rican delicacy. Plantains are also cut up and used in stews or are coarsely grated to make fritters. Local Puerto Rican cooks find that a variety of locally grown banana called Chinese banana is successfully used in recipes which call for green plantains.

Yams and sweet potatoes, yautia (a kind of taro), potatoes, corn, and breadfruit are also used in Puerto Rican cooking.

### Desserts

Puerto Ricans have many baked desserts. Some popular cakes include *ponque* (pound cake) and *sopa borracha* (sponge cake with rum sauce). They also bake cookies called *polvorones* and custards called flan.

Sweets are often deep fried in oil. Fritters, crullers, and small turnovers are enjoyed as snacks and desserts. Puerto Ricans also enjoy puddings as desserts. Rice flavored with coconut, spices, and milk is often the basis of the puddings. Stale bread or cakes are used in bread puddings. These puddings are sometimes topped with fresh fruit and flavored with Puerto Rican rum.

### Celebrations

Puerto Ricans celebrate traditional holidays such as Christmas, Easter, Thanksgiving, and New Year's Day as well as birthdays, weddings and baptisms.

In Hawai'i, Puerto Ricans take pride in their cultural heritage and the United Puerto Rican Association helps to keep traditions alive. The big event of the year is the celebration of *El Dia de los Tres Reyes*, Three Kings Day. In Puerto Rico, on this day, children find their shoes filled with presents, a reminder of the gifts borne by the wise men for baby Jesus. On this day the Hawaiian Puerto Rican community celebrates a special mass. Then a procession of trucks carrying musicians and dignitaries and the Three Kings, who walk the procession route accompanied by shepherds, leaves the church for the social hall. After reaching their destination the procession and the community enjoy a traditional Puerto Rican Christmas Party called *Trulla* with foods such as arroz con pollo, beans and rice, lechon asado, and of course, lots of singing and celebrating. Later, all children at the celebration receive a small gift from the Three Kings.

# Achiote Fat

**Makes 2 cups**
  1 pkg. (4 oz.) achiote seeds
  2 c. oil

In a small pan combine seeds and oil. Cook over low heat for 5 minutes or until oil has a rich red color. Strain and store in refrigerator.

To make a small amount, cover 1 Tbsp. of achiote seeds with boiling oil (about ¼ c.). Let it sit for a few minutes then strain.

Achiote seeds are available at Latin American grocery stores. In Hawai'i they are available at Tamashiro Market or in the Oriental food section of some large supermarkets.

# Banana Fritters

**Makes 10 - 12**

¼ c. butter, softened
1 clove garlic, mashed
2 medium plantains, peeled and
   grated (or green bananas)
oil for frying

Mix butter and garlic in a small bowl. Set aside.

In a medium sized heavy saucepan, heat oil for frying to 375 degrees. While oil is heating make small patties out of the grated plantains, using about ¼ c. at a time. Press firmly together. Using a slotted spoon, gently slip 2 or 3 patties into the hot oil. Fry until golden brown and turn once. Drain on paper towels.

Repeat until all patties are cooked. Brush one side of the patties gently with the garlic butter before serving. Serve as pupus or a side dish.

# Serenata
## Codfish Salad

**Serves 6**

| | |
|---|---|
| 1 lb. salt cod | 1 bunch watercress, cut into 1" pieces |
| 3 tomatoes, sliced | 1 lb. potatoes, boiled, peeled, and |
| 1 head lettuce, torn into | thinly sliced |
| pieces | 2 hard boiled eggs, peeled and thinly |
| 1 onion, thinly sliced into | sliced |
| rings | |

### Dressing:

| | |
|---|---|
| ½ c. oil | 2 Tbsp. wine vinegar |
| ½ c. soy sauce | 1 tsp. salt |

To prepare codfish: Soak salt cod in cold water at least 12 hours or overnight, changing water 2 or 3 times. Drain, rinse, and place in a pan. Add water just to cover and simmer, covered for about 30 minutes. Drain; flake into small pieces, removing any skin and bones. Cool and refrigerate for at least 2 hours.

**To assemble salad:**
Line a large platter with lettuce leaves and watercress. Place codfish in center and surround fish with alternate slices of

tomato, onion, potato, and egg slices. Pour dressing over salad and serve at once.

# Pasteles
### Bananas Stuffed with Pork

**Serves 6**

1 bunch of very green Chinese bananas
1 potato, grated
achiote oil
3-5 lbs. pork
1 green pepper, chopped
2 cloves garlic, minced
1 large onion, chopped
1 Tbsp. oregano
1 Tbsp. chili powder
2 (8 oz.) cans tomato sauce
cayenne pepper to taste
salt and pepper to taste
2 bunches cilantro (Chinese parsley), chopped
1 c. pitted black olives
ti or banana leaves

Peel and grate green bananas and potato (or process in a food processor). To make achiote oil, pour ¼ c. boiling oil over 1 Tbsp. achiote seeds. When oil has a rich red color, strain. Add achiote oil to grated bananas and potato a little at a time until they are pale orange in color. Season with salt to taste. Set aside.

**Filling:** Cut pork into tiny pieces. Saute in a pan; drain off any fat. In another saucepan heat left over achiote oil and saute green pepper, garlic, onion for a few minutes. Add seasonings, tomato sauce, parsley, olives and pork. Cook until pork bits are very tender. Cool.

**To prepare leaves:** Wash leaves and remove center rib from ti leaves. Soften leaves by pouring boiling water over them, or heat in a 200 degree oven just long enough to soften. If using banana leaves, cut into 10 inch pieces.

**To assemble:** Moisten leaf with a little gravy from the stew mixture. Place a large spoonful of the banana mixture on leaf; spread out into a rectangular shape. Place about 2 Tbsp. of strained meat filling along one side. Fold the leaf over, tucking ends in to form a neat package. Tie with string. Steam for 1 hour. Serve hot.

# Pescado en Escabeche
### Pickled Fish

**Serves 6**

3-4 lean fish
1 Tbsp. salt
3 Tbsp. lemon juice
2½ c. olive oil
½ c. olives

2 cloves garlic, crushed
1 c. vinegar
2 onions, sliced
2 bay leaves
1 tsp. peppercorns

Cut fish into fillets. Rub with salt and lemon juice. Heat ½ c. of olive oil in a skillet. Fry the fish. Remove fish from pan and and garlic, vinegar, onions, bay leaves, and peppercorns. Cook until onions are soft. Place fish and olives in a deep glass or porcelain dish. Pour remaining 2 cups of oil and the vinegar sauce over fish. Cover and refrigerate 24 hours before serving.


# Arroz Con Pollo
### Rice with Chicken

**Serves 6**

1 frying chicken, cut up
salt and pepper
¼ c. olive oil
½ c. stuffed olives
1 Tbsp. capers
1 onion, chopped
½ c. chopped green peppers

½ c. tomato puree
2 c. rice, washed
4 c. boiling water
1 c. green peas (cooked)
1 pimento, cut in strips

Season the chicken with salt and pepper and saute in olive oil until tender and golden brown. Add olives, capers, onion, green pepper and salt and pepper to taste. Cook for 5 minutes. Add tomato puree and rice. Stir and cook for 5 minutes. Add 4 cups boiling water. Cover and simmer until rice is tender. Put rice on a platter. Arrange chicken on top. Garnish with peas and pimento strips.

# Paella

**Serves 8**

1 lb. chicken breasts or thighs, deboned and cut into cubes
1 lb. lean pork or beef, cut in cubes
½ c. olive oil
½ lb. scallops
½ lb. shrimps, peeled and deveined
1 tomato, chopped
2 cloves garlic, crushed
2 c. rice, washed

1 7 oz. can minced clams
1 pkg. frozen artichoke hearts
1 pkg. frozen green beans or peas
2 tsp. salt
¼ tsp. saffron (or yellow food coloring)
3-3½ c. boiling chicken broth (canned or boullion cubes)
pimento, cut in strips

Heat olive oil in a large skillet or Dutch oven. Add chicken and pork. Saute until golden brown. Cover and simmer for 10-15 minutes. Add scallops and shrimp. Saute lightly for about 2 minutes. Stir in tomato, garlic, rice, clams (with liquid), vegetables, salt and saffron. Add boiling chicken broth. Cook, uncovered over high heat for 5 minutes, stirring occasionally. Cover and cook over medium heat (or bake in 350 degree oven until all the broth is absorbed) for 10-15 minutes. Garnish with pimento before serving.

# Sancocho
## Vegetable Stew

**Serves 6**

1 lb. beef (flank or chuck)
½ lb. lean pork
8 c. water
2 tomatoes, chopped
1 onion, chopped
1 green pepper, chopped
1 Tbsp. salt
1 can (8 oz.) tomato sauce

½ lb. yautia (taro), cubed
½ lb. pumpkin, cubed
½ lb. yams, cubed
½ lb. potatoes, cubed
1 green plantain, cut in 1 inch pieces
1 bunch cilantro (Chinese parsley), chopped

Cut beef and pork into 1 inch cubes. In a large saucepan, combine meats, water, tomatoes, onion, green pepper, and salt. Bring to a boil. Lower heat and simmer 1 hour or until meat is tender. Stir in remaining ingredients and simmer for 30 minutes or until vegetables are tender. Taste; add more salt and pepper if necessary.

# Pastelillos
## Pork Turnovers

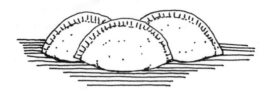

**Makes 36**

### Pastry

4 c. flour
2 tsp. salt
oil for frying

1 beaten egg
cold water or milk
2 Tbsp. shortening or lard

Sift together flour and salt. Add shortening, cutting into the flour with two knives or pastry blender until flour looks like coarse meal. Mix the egg with ½ c. water and add to flour, sprinkling a little at a time. When sufficient water has been added the dough is compact and pliable. Make several balls; cover and refrigerate until ready to use.

### Filling

1 lb. ground pork
2 oz. smoked ham
1 oz. salt pork
2 tomatoes, chopped
1 green pepper, chopped
1 onion, chopped

1 tsp. salt
2 Tbsp. oil
¼ c. sliced olives
1 Tbsp. capers
¼ c. raisins
2 hard boiled eggs, chopped

Grind ham and salt pork. Mix together with ground pork. Heat oil in skillet and cook pork, ham and salt pork with vegetables and salt until pork is cooked. Add olives, raisins, capers, and eggs to pork. Stir and remove from heat. Cool.

**To shape turnovers:** Roll out small balls of pastry on floured board with a rolling pin to a thickness of ⅛ inch or less. Cut circles 4 inches in diameter. Place a tablespoon or so of filling in center of dough. Fold over and seal edges with tines of a fork. Fry in deep fat. When turnovers rise to the top, pour fat over it with a spoon so pastry will puff up. Turn to brown other side. Drain on paper towels.

**Note:** To serve turnovers as pupus, cut dough into smaller circles, about 2½ inches in diameter.

# Sopa Borracha
## Cake with Rum Sauce

¾ c. cake flour  
1 tsp. baking powder  
¼ tsp. salt  
4 egg yolks  
½ c. sugar  
¼ c. boiling water  
1 tsp. vanilla

Grease an 8 inch square pan. Sift flour with baking powder and salt. In a small bowl, beat egg yolks with electric mixer until thick and lemon-colored. Gradually add sugar, beating well. Add boiling water and vanilla. Stir in the dry ingredients and pour immediately into pan. Bake for approximately 25 minutes at 350 degrees. Cool in pan for 10 minutes. Remove from pan. Pierce cake with fork in several places and pour rum sauce over it.

### Rum Sauce

2½ c. sugar   2 c. water   ¼ c. Puerto Rican rum

Combine sugar and water in a small saucepan. Cook to 210 degrees, stirring occasionally. Remove from heat; add rum.

# Arroz con Coco
## Coconut Rice Pudding

**Serves 4-6**

2 c. milk  
6 sticks cinnamon  
1 tsp. whole cloves  
1 2-inch piece of ginger, crushed  
1 qt. water  
1 c. rice (not instant or converted)  
2 c. coconut milk  
½ c. sugar  
1 tsp. salt  
½ c. raisins  
ground cinnamon

In a 1 quart saucepan, combine milk, cinnamon sticks, cloves, and ginger. Bring to a boil, lower heat, and simmer milk for 5 minutes. Remove pan from stove and let sit for at least 1 hour.

Strain the milk; discard cinnamon, cloves, and ginger. Bring water to a boil and cook rice, uncovered, for 5 minutes. Drain rice in a sieve and rinse with cold water. In a 2 or 2½ quart saucepan, combine coconut milk, spiced milk, sugar, and salt. Bring to a boil, stir in rice, cover pan, and simmer for 30 minutes.

Stir in the raisins; cook, covered, for another 10 minutes or until liquid is absorbed and rice is tender. Transfer pudding to a large serving bowl or individual dessert dishes and sprinkle with ground cinnamon. Serve at room temperature.

# Korean

## Introduction

To many people the mention of Korean food brings to mind only one thing, *kim chee*. But it encompasses a wide range of ingredients, flavors, and textures. Korean food is generally highly seasoned with spices such as red chili pepper, garlic, and green onions. However, many of the vegetable dishes and soups are not highly seasoned at all.

Korean food is basically healthy food, low in fat and high in nutritive value. A typical family meal consists of a soup of meat or fish with vegetables, cooked vegetables called *namul,* pan broiled fish or meat, rice, and *kim chee.* However, on special occasions or at parties a large variety of dishes is served. Koreans place a great importance on food and most have hearty appetites. Unlike the Chinese and Japanese, the Koreans are not tea drinkers. Instead, they drink grain teas, ginseng tea, or "rice water," the water that has been added to the residue remaining in the pot after rice is eaten.

Like the Chinese and Japanese, the first group of Korean immigrants came to Hawai'i as laborers to work on the sugar plantations. Coming in 1903, they were among the last Orientals to come as plantation workers. In recent years there has been a resurgence of Korean immigration to Hawai'i and other parts of the United States. The 1980 census figures report a 413% increase of Koreans in the ten year period since 1970. The reason for this increase in immigration is due partly to the change in biased immigration laws and partly to the Koreans' educational, political, and economic dissatisfaction in their country. Educational opportunities are limited in Korea and parents want a better life for their children. Secondly, Chung Hee Park's long presidency (1963-1979) caused repression and political unrest. Many Koreans, like immigrants before them, saw America as the land of opportunity, a place one could start a new life and have a chance at success. The new immigrants have opened many Korean restaurants, and, hence, Korean food has been discovered and loved by many people.

Korean food is easily prepared at home because its ingredients are basic and available in any supermarket. Popular Korean staples such as *kim chee* (pickled vegetables) and *taegu* (seasoned dried codfish) are found in jars in the deli section of all local supermarkets.

## Cooking Methods

Principal methods of Korean cookery are broiling or charcoal grilling, steaming, frying, and boiling. No special equipment is required, although a mortar and pestle for grinding sesame seeds comes in handy.

Koreans have a special cooking pot for the preparation of a dish called *sinsollo*. It is basically a chafing dish made out of metal (usually brass) with a small tube in the middle which holds burning charcoal. The pot is placed on the table and meats and vegetables are layered and simmered in a broth. Similar to the Japanese *shabu-shabu*, sinsollo is a special dish for special occasions, taking much preparation time. Today, electric woks or skillets can be used in place of the sinsollo pot.

## Seasonings

Hot and spicy are the two words that best describe Korean food. Red chili pepper is a basic seasoning. Fresh chili peppers, dried pepper flakes, and finely ground chili pepper powder are used. These are available in bulk from Korean grocery stores. In small quantities, cayenne pepper may be used as a substitute. Koreans often season already cooked food with various sauces and pastes called *jang*. *Kang jang* is a flavored soy sauce. *Kochu jang* is thick and fiery hot paste of soy bean paste (miso), sugar or honey, and chili pepper powder. Literally, *kochu* means pepper, and kochu jang is a peppery sauce. Generally, kochu jang is thinned with soy sauce or sometimes vinegar, but it is also used as it comes from the jar. It is used as sauce for dipping almost all foods as well as a hot sauce for plain rice.

Garlic, ginger, green onions, and chives are also basic to Korean cookery. These are the major seasonings for kim chee. Sesame seeds and sesame seed oil give a unique flavor to Korean dishes. Sesame seeds should be roasted and lightly crushed with a mortar and pestle or the back of a knife to achieve maximum flavor.

## Meat, Seafood, Soybean, and Eggs

Unlike other Orientals, Koreans are a beef eating people. Beef was probably introduced to Koreans during medieval times by Mongols who invaded the country. Beef ribs (kalbi), barbecued thin slices of beef (bul kogi), as well as hamburger, brisket, tongue and other organ meats are all popular dishes. Pork and chicken are widely used also.

In Korea seafood is an important part of the diet. All varieties of saltwater and fresh water fish such as carp and salmon are used along with shellfish and mollusks. Dried seafood is popular also. Dried cod fish or cuttlefish are combined with other ingredients to make spicy side dishes such as taegu.

From the sea Koreans also get seaweed which is high in vitamins and minerals. A clear, beef based seaweed soup is a must for a woman who has just given birth. The soup is served to her at least twice a day for a period of about three weeks. Laver, a type of seaweed that is commercially cultivated then pressed into thin sheets, is used extensively. It is often brushed with sesame oil and salt then grilled to a crisp and eaten. It is also used as a garnish for noodles or soups or wrapped around hot rice seasoned with kochu jang sauce.

Soybean products are another source of protein in the Korean diet. Tofu (soy bean curd) is used in many dishes. It is one of the main ingredients in the popular mandu (dumplings) and is often added to soups.

Eggs are not extensively used in Korean cookery; however, Koreans are fond of foods fried in an egg batter. Foods prepared in this manner are called chun. Meats, vegetables, or vegetables stuffed with ground beef or pork are prepared this way. Eggs are also used to make omelets and are fried thin and shredded for garnish.

## Vegetables

Vegetables are a large part of the Korean diet. They are usually cooked for only a short time so that they retain their crunchiness and vitamins. In Korea where winters are harsh, the people found it necessary to put up large quantities of vegetables for use during the winter months. Kim chee, highly seasoned pickled vegetables, was their way of preserving vegetables. It is a staple in the Korean diet, and today in Hawai'i all races enjoy this spicy hot relish. Kim chee is made out of cabbage, Chinese cabbage (won bok), turnips, or cucumber which is soaked in a mixture of salt, garlic, ginger, chives, and lots of chili pepper. Sometimes to enhance its flavor, dried fish, shellfish, or fish sauce are added. After aging for a few days the vegetables are ready to eat. The smell of kim chee is overwhelming to those unaccustomed to it, but its tastiness has gained many fans.

Fresh vegetables are enjoyed in a Korean version of salad called namul. Namul can be made out of any kind of vegetable.

Spinach, bean sprouts, watercress, cabbage, and cucumbers are frequently used. Basically, the vegetables in namul are blanched in hot water then chilled in a mild sauce of sesame seeds, oil, vinegar, salt or soy sauce. Vegetables prepared in this manner are crisp and crunchy and add contrast to meat and rice as well as eye appeal.

Vegetables are also cooked with meats or fish or dried fish. Chap chae is the Korean version of chop suey which uses a variety of vegetables using the stir-fry method of cooking. Dried vegetables such as fern shoots are cooked with bits of meat and are considered a delicacy. Koreans are also fond of taking vegetables that can be cut into rounds such as zucchini, lotus root, eggplant, and peppers, stuffing them with seasoned ground meats, and frying them in an egg batter.

### Rice and Noodles

White polished rice is the staple starch of the Koreans. For variety rice is sometimes cooked with other grains such as barley or beans. It is sometimes seasoned with salt, sesame seeds, and sesame oil and made into rice balls like the Japanese musubi. *Sangchu sam* is another version of Korean rice balls. Plain hot rice is served in leaf lettuce, seasoned with kochu jang sauce, and garnished with side dishes such as taegu, namul, and pieces of meat. The hot sauce, bland rice, and crisp cool lettuce make an interesting combination. Koreans also made a fried rice with meat and vegetables similar to Chinese fried rice, but with a sesame and garlic flavor.

Rice gruel *(jook)* is considered a snack or a bland food to be eaten during illness or convalescence. Rice is cooked in water seasoned with soy sauce, sesame oil, and ginger or garlic with bits of meat, fish, or chicken added. Jook is sometimes prepared with pinenuts, peanuts, walnuts, or other nuts and served with sugar or honey.

Koreans use yam noodle vermicelli (long rice) in their cooking in combination with meats and vegetables as in chap chae or in soups. *Kook soo* and cold kook soo are noodles in broth, garnished with sliced meats and vegetables. For this dish, thin Japanese somen noodles are used. The broth for this dish is sometimes seasoned with kim chee stock.

### Sweets

Like other Orientals, Koreans do not have desserts in the Western sense. Rather, their desserts are generally fruit or fruit in syrup, candied fruit or vegetables, and sweets made out of sticky mochi rice. Special sweets are generally reserved for occasions and holidays, with fruit ending the every-day meal.

Korean sweets include *songphyuns,* half-moon shaped pastries made out of rice flour and filled with sweet azuki (red bean) paste or sesame seed filling. *Yak pahb* or *yak sik* (honey rice), another sweet, is an exotic dessert which takes much time to prepare. Its base is mochi rice. Added to it are sugar and honey, pine nuts, chestnuts, sesame seeds, and dried fruits. Considered a holiday sweet, yak pahb is an unusual contrast of color and textures. Rich honey cakes called *yak kwa* are deep fried cakes which are rolled in a honey and water or juice mixture. These too are for festive occasions.

Not all Korean sweets take much preparation time. Sweets such as date balls and chestnut balls are merely mashed chestnuts and dates, combined with honey and cinnamon, and rolled into small balls.

### Celebrations

The most important celebration for Koreans is New Year's Day. They follow the lunar calendar as do the Chinese, but generally Koreans living in Hawai'i celebrate January first as their New Year. Birthdays, particularly the first and sixty-first birthdays, and weddings are also celebrated. The sixty-first birthday (actually the sixtieth because Orientals believe that a person is one year old when born) is celebrated by Japanese and Chinese as well. Its importance is based on the belief that people reaching that age are reborn and enter a second childhood because the cycle of years in the lunar calendar lasts for sixty years, after which one goes back to the beginning of the cycle.

Generally, a celebration menu will include chap chae (vegetables and noodles), mandu (dumplings), a variety of namul (cooked vegetables), sweets, as well as the always favorite bul kogi (barbecued meat) or kalbi (barbecued ribs), and of course kim chee. In addition, for the New Year's celebration, a traditional beef based soup with mochi called *d' ok guk* is prepared. Also at New Year's, some families prepare *nrum juk,* a time consuming but tasty skewered dish consisting of meat, kim chee, and vegetables skewered on long cocktail toothpicks which are dipped in an egg batter, then deep fried and served with vinegar and soy sauce.

In Korea Thanksgiving, which falls on November 15th, is an important celebration climaxing the autumn harvest. Koreans living in Hawai'i celebrate traditional Thanksgiving day, but along with turkey, pumpkin pie, and mashed potatoes, one is likely to find mandu, namul, and kim chee on the table.

# Kochu Jang
Chili Pepper Sauce

**Makes 1 qt.**

1 Tbsp. Hawaiian salt
½ c. boiling water
1 box dark brown sugar

½ c. fine chili pepper powder
1 (27 oz.) carton miso

Dissolve Hawaiian salt in boiling water. Place chili powder in a small bowl; add about 4 Tbsp. of the salt water. Add more salt water a spoonful at a time to form a paste the consistency of miso. You will probably use about 6 Tbsp. salt water.

Transfer the chili powder paste into a large mixing bowl. Add miso and brown sugar. Mix well; remove all lumps. Cover bowl and allow it to sit overnight at room temperature. The mixture will rise slightly and become darker in color.

Stir and pour into clean jars. Store in refrigerator. This sauce may be thinned with soy sauce and/or vinegar.

# Kim Chee

1 medium round cabbage  
¼ c. rock salt  
1 c. water  
1 Tbsp. sugar  
1 tsp. salt

1 inch piece of ginger, minced fine  
5 stalks green onion, chopped fine  
7-9 cloves garlic, crushed  
¼ c. crushed red pepper

Remove core from cabbage and slice into square pieces. Separate layers of cabbage leaves. Sprinkle with rock salt and pour water over cabbage. Let stand 45 minutes to 1½ hours, mixing occasionally. Squeeze out excess water. Place cabbage in a bowl. Mix rest of the ingredients with cabbage until all the red pepper is evenly distributed. Press kim chee in a jar; store in a warm place for ½ day. Refrigerate.

**Note:** Don't forget to lomi cabbage while it is being salted!

## Bean Sprout Namul
### Bean Sprout Salad

**Serves 6**

6 c. water  
2 Tbsp. salt  
1 Tbsp. oil  
2 tsp. sesame seeds

2 pkg. bean sprouts  
2 tsp. sesame seed oil  
2 stalks green onion, chopped

Bring water and salt to a boil and add sprouts. Cook for 1 minute. Rinse and drain well in a colander. Squeeze out water. Add all seasonings, mix well, and chill. Sprinkle with red pepper flakes before serving.

**Variation:** Saute ½ lb. lean ground beef. Add raw bean sprouts and seasonings. Cook until sprouts are done but still crisp.

# Sigumchi Namul
### Spinach Salad

**Serves 4**

| | |
|---|---|
| 1 lb. fresh spinach | 3 Tbsp. soy sauce |
| 1 Tbsp. vinegar | 1 Tbsp. sesame seed oil |
| ½ tsp. sugar | 1 Tbsp. sesame seeds, roasted |
| dash of pepper | 1 clove garlic, crushed |

Wash spinach and steam just until tender. Rinse in cold water and squeeze out water. Cut into 1 inch lengths. Combine all seasonings and add to the spinach. Chill.


# Taegu
### Seasoned Codfish

| | |
|---|---|
| 2½ Tbsp. honey | 1 pkg. (4 oz.) taegu fish (codfish) |
| ½ tsp. paprika | 2 tsp. sesame seeds, roasted |
| 3 tsp. sesame seed oil | ½ tsp. powdered chili pepper |

Shred codfish into small pieces. Mix all ingredients together, place in a jar, and let stand for a day before eating.


# Kogi Guk
### Beef Soup

**Serves 6**

| | |
|---|---|
| 1½ lbs. thin sliced beef | 6 c. water |
| 1 clove garlic, crushed | salt to taste |
| 1 Tbsp. soy sauce | 1 beaten egg (optional) |
| 2 tsp. black pepper | vegetables of your choice: turnip, |
| ¼ tsp. black pepper | cucumber, zucchini, watercress |
| 1 Tbsp. oil | 3 stalks green onion, cut in 1" pieces |

Mix together beef, garlic, soy sauce, sesame oil and black pepper. Heat oil in pan and cook beef until it is seared. Add water and simmer for about 1 hour. Skim off fat. Or at this point refrigerate the soup until fat hardens, then remove fat. Add more salt if necessary and sliced vegetables. Just before serving, add green onions and beaten egg.

# Korean Barbecue Sauce
### For Kalbi (short ribs) and Bul Kogi (barbecue meat)

**Sauce for 3-4 lbs. meat**

⅔ c. soy sauce          1 Tbsp. sesame seeds, roasted and ground
3 Tbsp. water           2 Tbsp. sesame seed oil
2 Tbsp. honey           2 cloves garlic, crushed
3 Tbsp. sugar           2 Tbsp. chopped green onions

Mix all ingredients together. Dip each piece of meat in the sauce and layer in a flat dish or pan. Pour more marinade on top. Marinate 4 hours before grilling over coals or broiling.

**Note:** For barbecue meat, purchase ready sliced meat, or slice your own, using any tender cut of meat such as chuck, sirloin, or flank steak. For bul kogi, buy short ribs with small bones. Score ribs so that they will not curl during cooking. This sauce may be used on chicken also.

# Saengsun Chun
### Fried Fish

**Serves 4**

salt                    1 lb. white fish fillets (Mahimahi, red
pepper                     snapper, cod)
⅓ c. flour              2 eggs, beaten          ¼-½ c. oil for frying

Cut fish into pieces about 2 inches square. Sprinkle with salt and pepper. Roll in flour and beaten egg and saute in hot oil until brown. Serve with Kochu jang vinegar sauce.

### Kochu jang vinegar sauce:

2 Tbsp. vinegar         1 Tbsp. sesame seeds, roasted and crushed
4 Tbsp. soy sauce       1 Tbsp. minced green onion
1 tsp. sugar            3 Tbsp. kochu jang sauce

# Green Pepper Chun

**Serves 6**

4-5 green peppers       1 stalk green onion, sliced
½ lb. ground beef       2 cloves garlic, minced
¾ tsp. salt             2 inch slice of tofu
1 tsp. sesame seeds     ½ c. flour
1 tsp. sesame oil       2 eggs beaten          oil

Remove seeds from peppers. Cut into quarters, or smaller pieces, depending on size of peppers. Combine beef, tofu, garlic, green onions, salt, sesame seeds, and sesame oil. Mix well.

Flour the insides of green peppers. Pat the meat mixture into the center depression. Dip the peppers into flour and then beaten eggs. Heat oil (about 2 Tbsp.) in a skillet. Saute the peppers meat side down until browned; turn over. Reduce heat and cook for about 5 minutes or until peppers are tender, but still crisp.

**Variations:** The same meat mixture may be used on cut zucchini, eggplant, or lotus root.

# Mandu
## Dumplings

**Makes 3 dozen**

36 mandu wrappers or won ton pi

**Filling:**

2 c. cabbage (or 1 c. cabbage and 1 c. rinsed kim chee)

½ block tofu
2 stalks green onions, chopped

1 pkg. bean sprouts
½ lb. ground beef or pork

1½ Tbsp. soy sauce
2 cloves garlic, chopped

1 tsp. salt
2 tsp. sesame seed oil

dash of pepper

Cook cabbage in ¼ c. water for about 5 minutes. Drain; squeeze out excess water using a cheesecloth or thin dish towel. Chop finely. Chop kim chee finely. Simmer bean sprouts in water for a few minutes. Rinse, drain, squeeze out water and chop finely.

Place tofu in cheesecloth or dish towel and squeeze out excess water. Combine all ingredients and mix well. Place about 1 Tbsp. of filling in center of mandu wrapper. Seal edges with a little water.

Boil water in a medium sized pot and drop a few dumplings at a time and cook until done . . . do not overcook. Remove with a slotted spoon.

Use as dumplings in soup. Make homemade stock or use Swanson's chicken broth (one can serves two). Garnish soup with chopped green onions, laver (seaweed), and thin strips of fried egg.

**To fry egg:** Add 1 tsp. water to each egg and beat. Heat a little oil in an omelet or crepe pan and fry thin sheets of egg. When cool, cut into very thin pieces.

Mandu can also be deep fried in hot oil and served as a side dish or pupu (appetizer).

# Chap Chae
## Mixed Vegetables with Meat

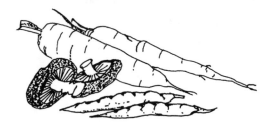

**Serves 4-6**

*½ lb. tender beef, such as loin or flank steak*
*2 pkg. long rice, soaked in warm water*
*6 dried mushrooms, soaked in warm water*
*1 clove garlic, minced*
*1 piece ginger about ½ inch slice, crushed*
*1½ Tbsp. soy sauce      ½ lb. green beans, in julienne slices*
*2 carrots, in julienne slices*
*1 round onion, cut in half and then sliced*
*2 stalks celery, thinly sliced          oil*
*2 tsp. sesame seeds                salt*

Slice beef in thin strips about 1½ inches long. Cut long rice into 2 inch lengths. Squeeze water from dried mushrooms and slice thinly. Chop all vegetables and set each one aside separately.

In a large pan, heat some oil and saute the beef with garlic, ginger, soy sauce, and sesame seeds. Cook until done, discard ginger, and set aside.

In the same pan, saute each vegetable separately in about 1 Tbsp. oil. Sprinkle lightly with salt and cook until vegetables are tender, but still crisp. Do not overcook. Saute the sliced mushrooms and drained long rice separately also, seasoning with a little salt.

Put all ingredients together in the pan and mix well. Taste; add more salt if necessary. Stir fry for a few minutes but do not overcook. Place on a large platter and garnish with more sesame seeds and thin strips of fried egg.

# Yak Pahb

## Honey Rice

**Serves 10**

4 c. mochi rice  
4 c. water  
1 c. dark brown sugar  
1 c. Chinese dried red dates, soaked in water 15 minutes, seeded and chopped  
2 pkg. dried chestnuts, boiled in 1 c. water, ½ c. sugar, ¼ tsp. cinnamon until almost tender  
¼ c. sesame seeds  
½ c. pine nuts  

⅔ c. honey  
¼ c. soy sauce  
⅓ c. sesame oil  
8-10 pitted prunes (optional)  

Soak mochi rice in 4 c. water for 2 hours; add a pinch of salt. Drain. Line a colander (metal) or steamer basket with cheesecloth; add rice and steam for 30 minutes, stirring once.

In a large bowl, mix sugar, honey, soy sauce, sesame oil, dates, chestnuts, sesame seeds, pine nuts, and prunes. Add rice; mix together well. Return to lined colander and steam for 3 hours, stirring several times from bottom to top, using a wooden spoon. Add more water to steamer as needed.

When rice is tender, place in an oblong cake pan (11 x 7 inches), or use several small foil pans and press down firmly. Cover with foil and cool. Cut into small pieces. Leftovers may be frozen and steamed again.

# Filipino

## Introduction

Although there are many Filipino people in Hawai'i, Filipino food is not as well known as Japanese and Chinese food. Filipinos are considered an Oriental people, yet they are Western in customs and tastes because of the Spanish influence in their country. The Spanish ruled in the Philippines for over three hundred years, until 1898 when the Philippines gained independence from Spain. The Spanish brought Christianity to the Filipinos and they left their influence in many foods. Some examples of the remaining Spanish influence in foods are the use of tomatoes, garlic, onions, and garbanzo beans in many dishes and the combining of more than one kind of food in one dish (such as cooking pork and chicken together in *adobo*). There are many Spanish dishes such as *paella* (seafood casserole), chicken *relleno* (whole stuffed chicken), and *leche flan* (custard). The Spanish influence in foods is seen particularly in the cooking of the Tagalog people from the vicinity of Manila.

But Filipino food also has Chinese and Malaysian influences from the Chinese and Maylay traders who were in the Philippines even before the Spanish. The Chinese influence is most evident in Ilocano cooking from the North. From the Chinese remain the use of many vegetables, noodles, dishes such as *lumpia* (similar to Chinese egg roll), and sweets made out of glutinous rice flour. The Malaysian traders' influence is seen in the cooking of the Visayan people in the South. Here there is heavy use of coconut and coconut milk in the cooking. So Filipino food can be describ-

102

ed as a mixture from other cultures as well as food using exotic (to us) ingredients such as banana blossoms, leaves of the horse-radish tree (marungay), and fern fronds (pako). Like the Puerto

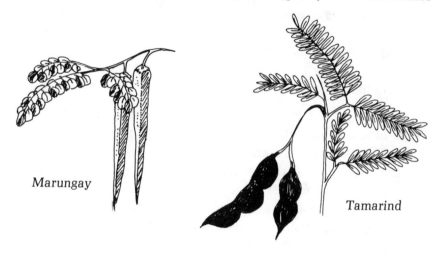

Marungay

Tamarind

Ricans, Filipinos sometimes use achiote seeds to give foods a reddish orange color.

Filipino cooking has some distinct characteristics: heavy use of garlic and onions, a tendency to cook many kinds of foods together, and many salty and sour flavored foods. Many Filipino dishes are flavored with vinegar or dipped in vinegar based sauces. Sometimes sour fruit such as green mango, *kalmansi* (Filipino lime), or tamarind are used in cooking to achieve the sour flavor. The salty flavor which Filipinos are fond of is achieved from fish paste called *bagoong* (ba-go-ong) and fish sauce called *patis*. These fish products are used in cooking as well as seasoning already cooked foods. Bagoong is sometimes eaten on plain cooked rice.

Filipinos arrived in Hawai'i beginning in 1906 and were the last large scale group of immigrant plantation workers to arrive in the islands. In recent years more Filipinos have arrived in Hawai'i and the new immigrants tend to live in closely knit communities. However, those who have been in Hawai'i for several years are spread throughout the islands in all communities. Local Filipinos, like other ethnic groups here, do not eat strictly

Filipino food. Yet many of their traditional dishes are loved and enjoyed not only for holidays, but for everyday meals.

There are only a few restaurants serving Filipino food in the islands. One of the most well known Filipino cafes is located in the older section of downtown Honolulu. In addition, there are a few small restaurants on the Leeward side of Oahu which serve Filipino food and confections.

### Cooking Methods

Frying, broiling, stewing, and boiling are the main methods of Filipino cooking. From the Spanish, they learned to saute in lard and olive oil. Stewing is used in many Spanish-originated dishes such as *pochero* and paella. Sometimes more than one cooking method is used in the preparation of one dish. Adobo is an example of multiple cooking methods. The meat in adobo is simmered first in its own marinade, then fried in oil until brown, and then cooked until tender.

### Meat/Fish

Pork is the most popular meat among Filipinos. It is cooked with fresh vegetables and used alone as in pork adobo. Adobo, which can be prepared with chicken, pork, or a combination of chicken and pork, could be called the most typical Filipino dish. Its main ingredients, vinegar and garlic, are typical of flavorings used by Filipino cooks. It has been said that adobo was originally a way of preserving meats without refrigeration for many days.

Chicken is widely used also. It is cooked with vegetables, made into stew, roasted with stuffing, or made into adobo. The Spanish influence is evident in two chicken dishes which are popular at feasts and special occasions. These are chicken relleno, a whole roasted chicken stuffed with pork sausage, spices, and eggs, and pochero. Pochero, a casserole of meat, vegetables, chickpeas (garbanzo), and potatoes, can also be made out of pork or beef.

Beef is used to a lesser extent than pork and chicken. But *kari-kari,* an oxtail casserole, and *bindonggo,* a tripe dish (beef stomach lining), are two favorites.

Fish and other seafood are widely used by Filipinos. Fish is fried, steamed, or cooked with vinegar. The distinctive fish paste, bagoong, and liquid sauce, patis, are important flavor additions to Filipino foods.

Bagoong and patis are always found in Filipino kitchens and they are used in cooking as well as a condiment or relish to flavor already cooked foods or plain hot rice. There are several varieties of bagoong and patis. Bagoong is a sauce of small fish or shrimps and salt which has been fermented. Anchovies, sardines, herring, scads, and shrimps are popular ingredients for bagoong. Usually a mixture of three parts fish or shrimp and one part salt is fermented from four to six months to make bagoong.

Patis, a clear yellowish-brown liquid sauce, is obtained from bagoong after it has been fermented. After the liquid is pressed out of bagoong, it is allowed to settle. Brine is sometimes added to the patis. Finally the patis is aged in large containers, then filtered and bottled. Both bagoong and patis can be found in large local supermarkets.

## Vegetables

Filipino cooks use a large variety of vegetables. Many of these vegetables are not available at the ordinary supermarket, but can be found in small specialty markets in the downtown Honolulu area or in neighborhood open markets. Hence, many Filipino families grow their own vegetables in backyard gardens. Tender shoots of sweet potato vines and leaves (kamote), squash flowers, banana blossoms, and leaves of

Banana
Blossom

Squash Flowers

the horseradish tree (marungay) are some popular ingredients. In addition, Filipinos use eggplant, bitter melon, squash, cabbage, swamp cabbage (ong choy), and string beans among other vegetables. Tomatoes and garlic are also heavily used.

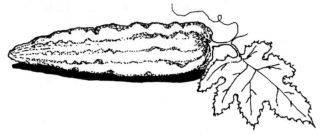

Filipinos most frequently cook their vegetables with some kind of meat or fish. However, they do not stir fry like the Chinese. Instead, their vegetables tend to be cooked with the meat in a liquid.

While ripe fruit is served as a dessert or snack, green fruit is often treated as a vegetable. Green papaya and green mango are often used in Filipino dishes. Like the Japanese and their tsuke-mono (pickled vegetable) and the Koreans and their kim chee (hot and spicy pickled vegetable), the Filipinos have a similar pickle dish called achara. Vegetables as well as green mango and green papaya are used in this side dish. One of the most popular Filipino dishes is chicken papaya, a kind of stew in which the green, cooked papaya resembles green squash in appearance, texture, and flavor.

### Starches

Filipinos eat rice as a staple in their diet. Sweet potatoes are sometimes served in place of rice and noodles (a Chinese influence) are also popular. The noodles, called pansit, are prepared in many different styles.

Glutinous rice flour (mochiko) is used by the Filipinos to make sweet desserts similar to the Chinese gau. Popular rice desserts include tupig which is made out of mochiko, brown sugar, and coconut milk and wrapped in banana leaves to cook, and bibinka, a baked pudding with ingredients similar to tupig.

## Desserts

Filipino people are fond of desserts; however, they do not usually serve desserts for daily meals. Sweets are mainly prepared for special occasions. Besides bibinka and tupig (mentioned in starch section), other favorites are *guinataan,* a coconut milk pudding with yams, taro, and bananas, *bunuelos,* rice flour dumplings fried and then rolled in sugar, and *flan,* a custard.

A popular liquid dessert and snack food among Filipinos is called *halo-halo.* Basically, this liquid sweet consists of crushed ice, sugar, and evaporated milk. To this any number of ingredients may be added, including shredded ripe fruit such as mango, papaya, or melon, crisp fried rice, jellies, and grated coconut. Literally, halo-halo means "a mixture," and that it is.

## Celebrations

The Filipinos are mainly Catholics and most of their celebrations are related to holiday observances such as Christmas and Easter, or occasions such as baptisms, weddings, birthdays, and funerals. Political holidays that are observed by some Filipinos are Jose Rizal Day (December 30), Commonwealth Day, (November 15), and Independence Day (June 12). Jose Rizal Day, a national holiday in the Philippines, is a tribute to Jose Rizal who is honored as the liberator of the Philippines from Spanish rule. Commonwealth Day is a celebration of the day the Philippines, a territory of the United States since the Spanish-American War, became a self-governing commonwealth in 1935. And Philippine Independence Day, June 12, 1898, marks the day that the Philippines became an independent nation.

On these celebration days, several elaborate dishes are prepared. More meat, poultry, and fish dishes appear than at a usual dinner and many sweets are served. Two favorite special dishes include *lechon,* or roasted pig, and chicken relleno, or roasted stuffed chicken.

# Fish Sinigang
A Soup

**Serves 4**

1 lb. white fish, cut into serving pieces
2 stalks green onion, cut in 1 inch pieces
3½ c. water          1 slice (½ inch) ginger, crushed
2 Tbsp. lemon juice          1 tomato, cut in wedges
salt and pepper to taste
1 c. marungay leaves or kamote (sweet potato) tops

Bring fish, water, onion, ginger, and tomato to boil in a pot. Reduce heat and simmer 10 minutes. Add salt, pepper, lemon juice, and marungay leaves. Cook only until leaves are wilted.

# Achara
Pickles

**Serves 3-4**

¼ c. cider vinegar          1 large green papaya -about 4 cups
½ tsp. salt          1 red chili pepper, minced
1 tsp. sugar          1 Tbsp. ginger, grated

Peel papaya and remove the seeds. Cut into very fine strips. Mix all ingredients together. Put in a clean jar and refrigerate overnight. Serve as a side dish.

# Lumpia

**Makes 24**

1 Tbsp. oil

2 cloves garlic, minced

1 c. string beans, slivered

1 small onion, minced

salt and pepper to taste

¾ lb. ground pork or beef

1 small carrot, shredded

½ pkg. bean sprouts

1 pkg. lumpia wrappers

oil for frying

Heat oil in saucepan. Saute garlic and onion. Add ground pork, salt and pepper. Brown well; drain off fat. Add vegetables and stir fry until just tender. Drain and cool.

Put 1-2 Tbsp. of filling in center of wrapper. Fold edge closest to you over filling. Tuck in the two ends. Fold like an envelope. Moisten edge with a little cornstarch mixed with water to seal. Heat oil to 375 degrees and deep fry until browned. Serve with lumpia sauce.

## Lumpia Sauce:

¼ c. soy sauce

¼ c. vinegar

2 green onions, chopped

2 Tbsp. roasted sesame seeds

dash of red pepper flakes

2 cloves garlic, minced

# Chicken or Pork Adobo

**Serves 4-6**

2 bay leaves

½ c. wine vinegar

10 whole peppercorns

3 Tbsp. oil

3 lbs. chicken or pork, cut up

salt and pepper to taste

½ c. white wine or beer

1 clove garlic, minced

Season chicken or pork with salt and pepper. Place in a pan. Mix together all other ingredients, except oil and pour over the chicken or pork. Bring to a boil. Simmer with cover slightly off until meat is tender and all liquid has evaporated. Add oil to the pan and saute meat until all sides are brown.

# Chicken Papaya with Marungay

**Serves 6**

1 tsp. salt
2 Tbsp. oil
1 slice ginger, crushed
1 medium onion, sliced
water

1 chicken (about 3 lb.) cut up
2 medium sized green papayas
2 c. marungay leaves (leaves of
   horseradish tree)

Season chicken with salt and brown in hot oil. Add ginger and onion and saute until onion is transparent. Cover chicken with water (about 4 c.) and simmer for 1 hour or until chicken is tender. Peel papayas, remove seeds and slice into 2½ inch pieces. Add to chicken and cook until papaya is tender but not mushy. Add the marungay leaves; cover pot and turn off heat. Let stand for a minute. Serve immediately.


# Morcon
## Beef Roll

**Serves 6**

1 small can Vienna sausage, drained and cut into strips
10 oz. mild Portuguese sausage, cut in half lengthwise
2 hard cooked eggs, halved lengthwise

2 Tbsp. lemon juice
¼ c. soy sauce
2 Tbsp. oil
1 can consomme
1 c. white wine
1 bay leaf, crushed

1 flank steak, about 2 lbs
2 cloves garlic, crushed
1 carrot, cut in strips
¼ c. chopped sweet pickles
6 peppercorns, crushed
½ tsp. salt

Pound the steak with the back of a knife. Marinate the steak in lemon juice, soy sauce, and garlic. Arrange Vienna sausage, Portuguese sausage, eggs, carrot, and pickles on top of the steak and roll with the fibers lengthwise. Tie with string. Brown meat in hot oil on all sides. Combine remaining ingredients and pour over meat. Cover, bring to a boil, then simmer for 1½ hours or until tender. Slice and arrange on a platter. Pour on the pan juices.

# Pochero
## A Stew

**Serves 4-6**

water
salt
pepper
1 onion, sliced
1 potato, cubed
1 Tbsp. sugar

1 large chicken, cut into small pieces

1 clove garlic, minced
3 green bananas, sliced 1 inch thick
½ c. cooked garbanzo beans (chick peas)
½ small cabbage, coarsely shredded

Put cut up chicken in a pan, cover with water and cook until tender. Add onion, garlic, potato, and garbanzos. Season with salt and pepper and cook until the potatoes are almost tender. Add the bananas and cabbage and cook about 10 minutes, or until both are tender. Add sugar and more salt if necessary.

**Variation:** 2 lbs. beef may be substituted for chicken.

# Pinacbet
## Vegetables with Shrimp

**Serves 4**

1 c. long beans, cut in 2½ inch lengths (or use okra)
2 bittermelon
4 long eggplants
1 Tbsp. bagoong
salt

2 ripe tomatoes, cut in quarters
1 slice ginger, crushed
1 c. water
¼ c. dried shrimps

Slice bittermelon lengthwise and remove seeds. Cut into 2½ inch lengths. Cut eggplants into 2½ inch lengths. Bring water and bagoong to a boil. Add eggplant and bittermelon. Then add tomatoes, ginger, and long beans. Cover and simmer vegetables in the sauce for 15 minutes. Gently toss vegetables and add dried shrimps. Simmer for another 5 minutes. Add salt to taste.

**Variations:** There are many ways of preparing this dish. Pork or pork rind may be used in place of dried shrimp. Onions, kamote (sweet potato) shoots, or other vegetables may be added.

# Apritada
## Pork with Pimento and Garbanzo Beans or Peas

**Serves 4**

1 lb. pork, sliced

3 cloves garlic, crushed

1 tomato, sliced

½ round onion, sliced

2 tsp. achiote seed,
 crushed and soaked in ¼ c. water

1 small can pimento

1 (16 oz.) can garbanzo beans or
 peas (use frozen peas if desired)

1 Tbsp. soy sauce

salt and pepper to taste

Fry pork with garlic until it is cooked. Add tomato and onion and cook until onion is soft. Add achiote seeds with water. Cook 5 minutes. Add pimento and beans or peas. Season with soy sauce, salt and pepper. Cover and simmer until pork is tender.

# Balatong
## Mungo Beans and Pork

**Serves 4**

water

5 oz. mungo beans (½ pkg.)

1 c. pork, sliced

3 cloves garlic, crushed

2-3 Tbsp. patis

1 tomato, sliced

½ round onion, sliced

2 c. marungay leaves or bitter
 melon leaves

Boil mungo beans in water about 5 minutes. Drain and remove skin. Place beans in a saucepan and cover with water again. Cook until soft, about 5 minutes. Do not drain. Set aside.

In another pan, fry pork with garlic until brown. Add patis, tomato, and onion. Cook until onion is soft. Add mungo beans (with water); cook about 3 minutes. Add greens and cook a few minutes longer.

# Leche Flan
## Custard

**Serves 6**

1 can (large) evaporated milk with enough milk added to make 2 cups
¼ c. water
8 egg yolks
1 tsp. vanilla
1 c. dark brown sugar
1 c. sugar

In a small saucepan, cook brown sugar and water over medium heat, stirring constantly until sugar carmelizes. Quickly pour into a quart mold or 8 inch square pan. Tilt mold to cover sides and bottom evenly.

Scald the milk. Blend together the egg yolks, sugar, milk, and vanilla. Pour into mold. Place in a larger pan that has been half filled with hot water and bake at 350 degrees for 1 hour or until a knife inserted into the custard comes out clean.

# Bibinka

**Makes 1 9x13 inch pan**

1 c. brown sugar
½ c. white sugar
dash of salt
2 eggs
¼ c. melted butter
banana leaves
1 10 oz. pkg. mochiko
1 Tbsp. baking powder
1 large can evaporated milk
1 c. shredded coconut
sesame seeds (optional)

Line a 13 x 19 inch pan with wilted banana leaves (wilt leaves by pouring boiling water over them) or grease pan lightly. In a large bowl mix mochiko, sugars, salt, and baking powder. Beat eggs, evaporated milk, and butter together and pour into dry ingredients and mix well. Add coconut. Pour into pan and sprinkle with sesame seeds. Bake 45 minutes to 1 hour at 350 degrees. Cool and cut into bars.

# Samoan

## Introduction

The only sizeable group of Polynesian people to migrate to Hawai'i, the Samoans are now a significant part of Hawai'i's population. Unlike other immigrants to Hawai'i they did not come as plantation workers. And because most of the Samoans come to Hawai'i from American Samoa and are considered American citizens, they can enter the state without complicated immigration procedures. The first Samoans arrived around 1919 when the Mormon Temple at Laie was built. Later, when the naval base at American Samoa was closed, many Samoans were transferred to Hawai'i as military personnel or dependents. Today there are approximately 13,000 Samoans residing in Hawai'i, most of them on Oahu.

Samoan people living in Hawai'i, like other ethnic groups, do not eat strictly Samoan food. But they do enjoy their native foods along with a varied, multi-ethnic diet, typical of Hawai'i's people. While some of the ingredients used and preferred by Samoans are available in any major Hawai'i supermarket, there are a few small stores which carry specialty items such as salt beef (sold by the keg), imported canned corned beef from New Zealand, and New Zealand crackers. In addition, the Samoan stores stock staples such as green bananas, fresh coconuts and taro.

Samoan food can be characterized as being plain, and, if seasoned, the main seasonings consist of coconut milk, onions, and salt.

## Cooking Methods

Like the Hawaiians, Samoans tend to use baking, boiling or steaming, and broiling to prepare their food. They prepare an oven called an *umu,* which is similar to the Hawaiian's imu. Unlike the Hawaiian underground imu, the umu is built above the ground with a shelter over it. Smooth stones collected from streams and beaches are heated and leaves and food are placed above and below them. More leaves are used to cover the food completely.

## Meat/Fish

Samoans favor pork over any other kind of meat. Pork, usually a small roasted pig, is a must at any celebration. Like the Hawaiians, Samoans also eat a dish similar to laulau. This consists of pork and taro leaves (lū'au) baked in a banana leaf wrapper.

Salt beef *(povi masima)* is also loved by Samoans. Salt beef is brisket of beef soaked in brine. It is similar to corned beef and is prepared much the same way. Salt beef is boiled in a pot of water. The water is changed two or three times, depending on the saltiness of the beef. After the meat is tender vegetables such as cabbage are added.

Canned corned beef is another meat Samoans favor. The New Zealand corned beef which they prefer is fattier than the standard canned corned beef which is from South America.

Canned corned beef is usually sauted with cabbage or onions.

Chicken is also used by Samoans. It is often baked or grilled over hot coals. Sometimes it is cooked in an umu.

Samoans eat both raw and cooked fish. Raw fish may be prepared with chopped onions, salt, and coconut milk. Sometimes chopped cucumbers and tomatoes are added. This Samoan style raw fish is similar to the Hawaiian's lomi salmon. Fish is often baked wrapped in ti leaves. Sometimes the fish is cooked whole, including the entrails. Coconut milk is often used as the seasoning for baked fish.

Octopus, boiled to softness and then seasoned with coconut milk and onions and salt, is another seafood favorite. Lobster, crab, and other shellfish are also boiled and served with a coconut milk, lime juice, and salt water sauce called *miti*. Canned fish such as salmon, mackeral, and sardines combined with onions is also popular with Samoans.

## Vegetables

Except for the leaves of the taro *(talo)*, Samoans do not use green vegetables in large amounts. The taro leaves are prepared with coconut milk and the result is called *palu sami*. Taro leaves are also eaten boiled or baked in bundles. Cabbage, celery, and onions are sometimes cooked with corned beef or slices of beef to make a sort of chop suey.

**Starches**

 Taro is a staple starch of Samoans. The corm of the taro is peeled, then baked or boiled. Sometimes coconut milk is added to taro for seasoning. Unlike Hawaiians, Samoans do not make poi out of taro.

Breadfruit *(ulu)* and bananas *(fa'i),* although classified as fruit, are used as sources of starch in the Samoan diet. These

fruits, when used in the green stage, have a high amount of carbohydrate (starch). Both breadfruit and banana are used green by the Samoans.

Cooked breadfruit resembles potato in flavor. A special breadfruit dish, called *taufolo,* is made for special occasions. For this dish breadfruit is baked in its skin. Then it is mashed and coconut milk added for flavor.

Besides breadfruit, bananas, and taro, rice, sweet potatoes, and bread are sources of starch in the Samoan diet.

**Fruit**

 Tropical fruits such as bananas, mangos, pineapple, papayas, and citrus fruit are enjoyed by Samoans. Fruit is usually eaten as a snack. Samoans make poi out of fruit rather than taro. Pineapple, melons, bananas, and other fruit are mashed and offered as a dessert or snack.

The coconut is very important in Samoan cooking. It is used for all purposes. The juice of young coconuts, a clear, sweet liquid, is used for drinking and the soft meat of the young coconut, called "spoon meat," is given to babies. The meat of the

dark shelled, mature coconut is grated and squeezed (with water added) to make coconut cream and coconut milk. Coconut cream and coconut milk are basically the same, the only difference being the amount of water added to the grated coconut. Traditionally, Samoans grate coconut meat on a grater attached to a stool or chair. The blade of the grater may be made out of metal or a notched coconut shell. The coconut is cracked into halves, but the meat is not removed from its shell. The coconut is then grasped firmly in the hands while the person sitting on the stool scrapes the meat over the grater. The grated meat falls into a

bowl or pan placed beneath the grater. The meat is then squeezed and strained.

Coconut milk has a high fat content, but is low in protein. It is a good source of iron and phosphorus, but is a poor source of vitamin C. Coconut milk is used by Samoans to season fish, chicken, vegetables, and fruit as well as to make dipping sauces. However, the coconut meat itself is rarely used because it is considered too dry. Commercially prepared frozen coconut milk is used by some local Samoans in place of the freshly grated and squeezed milk. And canned coconut cream, which is richer and thicker, is available at Samoan grocery stores and in some large supermarkets.

## Celebrations and Customs

Samoans love a celebration. A wedding, birthday, and traditional Christian holidays such as Christmas and Easter are celebrated with feasting. Pork is usually the main dish at such a feast. Often a whole suckling pig will be prepared. Chicken, taro, and breadfruit as well as raw fish and octopus or squid with coconut milk are traditional fare. An umu or above-ground oven is often built for the cooking of these foods.

In Samoa during the New Year's celebration, families go to surrounding neighborhoods and sing and dance to entertain their friends and neighbors much as carolers entertain during the Christmas season in the United States. In return the entertainers are given food and drink by their neighbors. In predominantly Samoan neighborhoods of Hawai'i, this tradition is carried on, but to a lesser degree.

Another special celebration for Samoans is White Sunday, which occurs in October. White Sunday is a special day for the children because on this day their elders honor them. Everyone wears white on this day, and children are usually given gifts of white clothing. Traditionally, Samoan adults and children eat separately, the adults always eating before the children. But on this one day, the children are allowed to feast before their elders.

Intensely patriotic, the Samoan community in Hawai'i celebrates Flag Day with feasts, songs, and dances. Flag Day commemorates the time when American Samoa came under the American flag. On this day Samoans wear their traditional clothes, serve traditional foods, and enjoy their native culture.

# Pe'e Pe'e
### Coconut Cream

COCONUT CREAM is a basic ingredient in preparing Samoan foods. Richer than coconut milk, canned coconut cream is available in Hawai'i at Samoan grocery stores or in some large supermarkets.

To make coconut cream from fresh coconuts, select mature nuts with firm but not dry meat. Remove the husk, pierce the eyes of the coconut, drain the liquid. Crack the nut and remove the meat. Peel off the brown skin and grate the meat with a grater or process in a food processor. Place the grated coconut in a thin dish towel or in cheese cloth. Add water, a little at a time and squeese out as much liquid as possible. Refrigerate.

Dried, unsweetened coconut may be substituted for fresh coconuts. To 1½ c. dried coconut, add 1 cup of extra rich milk or half and half. Simmer for 10 minutes; do not boil. Let stand until cool and strain through a dish towel or cheese cloth.

# Banana Poi

**Serves 4**
> 2 c. very ripe bananas, mashed
> 2 Tbsp. lemon juice
> 1 c. coconut cream

Mash bananas until a smooth paste is formed. Add the lemon juice. Gradually add the coconut cream, stirring constantly. Chill and serve in glasses.

# Baked Breadfruit with Coconut Cream

**Serves 6**

> 1 medium breadfruit, just beginning to soften
> 3-4 coconuts or 1½-2 c. canned coconut cream

Prepare coconut cream out of the grated coconuts (see recipe for Coconut Cream). Bake breadfruit in 350 degree oven for 1 hour or until it is soft. Cut in half; remove skin and core. Mash the pulp until it is smooth. Heat the coconut cream until it curdles and pour over the mashed breadfruit. Serve as a vegetable or dessert.

**Note:** Baked breadfruit may be served with butter in place of coconut cream.

# Palu Sami
### Taro Leaves Baked in Coconut Cream

**Serves 6**

| | |
|---|---|
| 1 tsp. salt | 2½-3 lbs. taro leaves |
| ¼ c. water | 2 c. coconut cream |
| banana leaves | 6 breadfruit leaves (or foil) |

Wash taro leaves, removing tough stems and veins. If leaves are large, divide into pieces. Wash and dry banana and breadfruit leaves. Add salt and water to coconut cream.

Arrange about 10 taro leaves in the palm of the hand, forming a cup. Pour in about ⅓ c. of the coconut cream into the leaves and fold the leaves over each other to keep in the cream. Place the taro leaf bundle on a banana leaf about 6" x 8" and overlap the banana leaf edges. Place this bundle on a breadfruit leaf (or heavy foil) and make another bundle, tucking in the stem of the breadfruit leaf. Steam for 2 hours, or bake in the oven at 350 degrees for 2 hours.

Discard the breadfruit and banana leaves and serve the bundle as a cooked vegetable.

# Raw Fish, Samoan Style

**Serves 4**

1 onion, minced
salt

1 lb. sliced raw fish
1 c. coconut milk

Slice raw fish and sprinkle with salt to taste. Add minced onions and coconut milk. For variety, chopped tomatoes and cucumbers may be added.

# Octopus in Coconut Milk

**Serves 4**

salt
1 c. coconut cream
1 small onion, chopped

1 octopus, fresh or cooked
ti or banana leaves (optional)

If using fresh octopus, cook until tender in boiling water. Slice octopus and place on ti or banana leaves. Season with salt and chopped onion. Pour coconut cream over octopus. Fold over the leaves and wrap the package in heavy duty foil. Bake in 350 degree oven for 10-15 minutes.

# Samoan Baked Fish

**Serves 4**

salt
1 c. coconut cream
ti leaves

1 mild flavored fish, with head and tail

Clean fish but do not remove tail and head. Rub inside and out with salt. Line a baking dish with clean ti leaves. Place fish on the leaves and pour coconut cream over it. Cover with more ti leaves and bake in 350 degree oven for 1 hour or until fish is tender.

# Samoan Style Baked Chicken

Traditionally this dish was baked in an umu, but is now usually baked in the oven.

salt                              1 whole chicken, about 3 lbs.
foil                              ti leaves

Sprinkle the chicken inside and out with salt. Wrap in ti leaves and then in foil. Bake in a 350 degree oven for 1-1½ hours. Unpeeled breadfruit may be baked in the same oven and served as a starch.

# Povi Masima
## Salt Beef

POVI MASIMA is salted beef brisket, similar to corned beef. It is available at Samoan grocery stores.

*To prepare:* Wash salt beef and place in a large pot; cover with water. Bring to a boil and simmer about two hours. Change the water about two or three times during the cooking period to get rid of excess salt. When beef is tender, add cut up cabbage and cook until cabbage is done. Or add cut up green papaya that has been peeled and seeded.

# Samoan Chop Suey

**Serves 4-6**

1 bundle long rice, soaked in water and cut in 2" pieces
2 Tbsp. oil                       1 small onion, sliced
1 clove garlic                    1 lb. chuck steak, sliced thin
2 carrots, sliced                 2-3 stalks celery, sliced
soy sauce to taste                ½ small head cabbage, chopped

Heat oil in a skillet and saute garlic and onion. Add beef and brown. Add long rice and add soy sauce to taste. Add vegetables and cook until they are tender. (A little water may have to be added to keep the long rice from sticking to the pan.)

**Note:** Canned corned beef may be substituted for sliced beef.

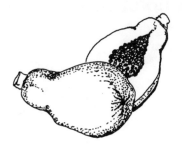

# Esi Fafao
Stuffed Papaya

**Serves 4**

1 onion, chopped
½ c. bread crumbs
1 lb. ground beef
2 Tbsp. milk

1 green papaya (large)
1½ tsp. salt
2 eggs
½ tsp. pepper

Wash and peel papaya. Cut off stem end and clean out seeds using a spoon. Chop onions and shred bread crumbs. Mix onions and bread crumbs with the beef, eggs, milk, salt, and pepper. Stuff papaya with beef mixture. Rub papaya with a little cooking oil and sprinkle with salt and pepper. Place in a pan with a cover, or cover pan with foil. Bake at 350 degrees for 45 minutes. Remove cover and continue to bake about 15 minutes.

# Southeast Asian

## Introduction

The end of the Vietnamese conflict in 1975 brought a large number of new immigrants to Hawai'i . . . the Southeast Asians. Vietnamese and Thai refugees opened small, unpretentious restaurants and Southeast Asian food quickly became another part of Hawai'i's food legacy.

Thailand is bordered by China on one side and India on the other side, and Thai food shows the influence of the two neighboring countries. Obvious Chinese influence can be seen in stir-fried vegetables with pieces of pork or chicken, crisp fried noodle dishes, and fish seasoned with ginger and soy sauce. The Indian influence on Thai food is apparent in the use of curry and other spices. Historically, Thailand was important as a center of trade between Asia and Europe, and the various ethnic groups introduced many foods to the Thai that are now an important part of their cuisine. The Portuguese are credited with the introduction of chili pepper, which accounts for a basic flavoring in Thai food. The Portuguese influence is also seen in some desserts. Tomatoes were also introduced by European traders and tapioca, now a staple in the Thai diet, came from Central America. Coffee, the official Thai beverage, came to the country by way of Java in the East Indies. There are several very popular Thai restaurants in Honolulu now.

Ethnically, the Laotians are Thais too, and their food is quite similar. However, unlike the Thais the Laotians have no curry dishes. One unique difference between Laotians and other South-

125

east Asians is that Laotians prefer sticky or glutinous rice rather than the conventional white fluffy rice. The sticky rice is steamed in woven baskets then taken with the fingers and eaten with other foods. The wad of sticky rice is used as a sort of "pusher" to get the food together and sop up the juices. Laotians do not use chopsticks or other eating utensils, depending mainly on fingers and sticky rice to get food into their mouths.

Vietnamese food is similar to Thai food, but it is not as highly seasoned. Like Thai food it is highly influenced by the Chinese. The Vietnamese tend to eat plain white rice rather than mixing the rice with other foods, and they are the only people in Southeast Asia who eat with chopsticks. While the Vietnamese have many stir-fried dishes, their food is more subtle in flavor than Chinese food. The French, who occupied Vietnam for most of the past century, also had influence on Vietnamese food. French bread, croissants, cheese, and coffee are enjoyed by the Vietnamese.

## Cooking Methods

As in other Oriental cookery, Southeast Asian cooking entails a maximum amount of preparation time and a fairly minimum actual cooking time. The cooking methods of simmering, stir-frying, barbecuing, and steaming and the equipment, are simple.

The wok and the multi-tiered bamboo steamer, which are popular in Chinese cooking, are basic equipment with the Southeast Asians also. In addition, mortars and pestles are traditional kitchen tools and come in all sizes. Mortars are of earthenware with a weighted base and pestles are carved out of wood. They are used mainly for pounding and grinding spices. While a blender or food processor simplifies this chore, sometimes only a small amount of spice needs to be ground, making the mortar and pestle more convenient.

A most important cooking aid in Southeast Asia is the banana leaf. Growing wild in the countries, it is used like aluminum foil. Foods are steamed in it and containers are made from it. In Hawai'i banana leaves are plentiful, but elsewhere, aluminum foil may be substituted.

### Seasonings

Some seasonings are virtually unique to Southeast Asian cookery. The most important are fish sauce, lemon grass, and galingale, also known as *laos* or *ka*. Fish sauce is the most dominant flavoring used. The sauce, which is made out of small salted fermented fish or shrimp, is known as *nam pla* in Thailand, *nuoc mam* in Vietnam, and *padek* in Laos. The fish sauces take the place of salt and are rich in protein and vitamin B. Nam pla and nuoc mam are available in Oriental grocery stores, but Laotian padek is not available in this country. Anchovies can be used as a substitute for padek.

The Thais have a basic hot sauce that appears on every table and at all meals. It is called nam prik. Basically, nam prik sauces are concocted out of dried shrimp or fish, shrimp paste, garlic, chilies, nam pla, lime juice, and sugar. There are as many versions of nam prik as there are cooks. The sauce is used as a dipping sauce or accompaniment for all food.

Many herbs which are exotic to Western cooks are necessary ingredients in Southeast Asian cookery. Lemon grass, or citronella, is an herb with long green leaves, a woody stalk, and a bulbous base. It gives a subtle sour or lemony flavor. Fresh lemon grass is easily grown in a warm climate and it is available in some Oriental grocery stores. It is also available in dry or powdered form.

Galingale or ka is a rhizome of the ginger family. The dried root is sold whole or in powdered form in Oriental stores specializing in Southeast Asian foods. It has a tart flavor and is most often used in cooked sauces or in soups.

Less exotic seasonings used in Southeast Asian cooking include fresh ginger, coriander (also known as cilantro or Chinese parsley), fresh mint, chili peppers, garlic, and shallots. While these ingredients are commonly used in many Oriental dishes,

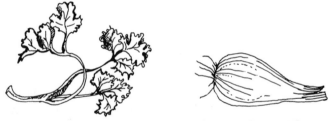

the use of coriander root is unique to Thai cookery. The roots are usually pounded and ground into a paste with a mortar and pestle and used to season various dishes.

Curry is an important seasoning in Thai cookery. There are three basic types of curry. Yellow curry was most likely introduced to the Thais by the Indians. It is a milder version of Indian curry. Red and green curries are more Thai in origin. Red curry is hot and made from red chili peppers, garlic, lemon grass, ka, and red onions. This curry is most often used for beef curries. Green curry gets it color from green chili peppers and herbs. Green curry is somewhat sweeter than red curry and is often used with poultry. All types of curries are generally diluted with coconut milk before the addition of meats or vegetables. Commercially prepared curry pastes are available in Oriental grocery stores, but they are easily prepared at home with the use of a mortar and pestle or food processor.

Coconut milk is very important in Southeast Asian cooking. The coconut meat itself is used only for desserts and decoration. Coconut milk called for in recipes is not the juice of the coconut itself. It is the juice which is extracted from the meat of the coconut after it has been soaked in boiling milk or water. Coconut milk can be made from fresh coconuts or from dry unsweetened coconut which is available in health food stores. Usually milk is pressed twice from a coconut. The first pressing is referred to as "thick" coconut milk while the second pressing is known as "thin" coconut milk. Coconut milk keeps in the refrigerator for about two days, or it may be frozen.

## Meat, Poultry and Seafood

Essentially, the Southeast Asians are a fish-eating people. Meat and poultry are reserved for special occasions. When meat is served it is not served in hunks as in Western culture, but in small pieces stretched with coconut milk sauces or vegetables and mounds of rice. Chicken is more widely used than beef or pork, perhaps because it is less expensive. Duck is also used.

Thais and Laotians are fond of a sour flavored pork sausage which they eat raw. It is heavily seasoned with hot chilis, ginger, peanuts, and onions and is similar to the Chinese sausage, lup chong. While Americans are cautioned against eating raw pork, the heavy seasoning and spices seem to make this raw pork sausage safe to eat.

Fish and other seafood are plentiful in Southeast Asia and are the main source of protein. Freshwater and saltwater species of fish are used as well as shrimp, prawns, crab, lobster, squid, and oysters. Fish is prepared in many ways. Although it is most often fried or steamed whole, it is also made into curry dishes and stir-fried with vegetables. Fish soups flavored "hot and sour" are a tradition in Southeast Asia, as are spring rolls stuffed with crab, shrimp, and vegetables.

### Vegetables

Vegetables are a main part of the Southeast Asian diet and they appear at every meal. Salads of raw vegetables as well as meat-vegetable stir-fried dishes are popular. In their native countries the Southeast Asians use all sorts of edible flowers, shoots, and leaves which grow wild. Citrus leaves and mango leaves are used in salads. The Laotians even have a soup called furr, which contains along with pork, noodles, and garlic, the leaves of the marijuana plant.

In this country a variety of vegetables can be used in Southeast Asian cookery: watercress, Chinese cabbage, eggplant, mustard greens, cucumbers, tomatoes, spinach, and various kinds of lettuce are only some of the frequently used vegetables. The salads served by the Southeast Asians often contain bits of beef, chicken or seafood along with the vegetables and make a delightful lunch.

One popular and well known Vietnamese dish is cha-gio (spring roll) which consists of vegetables and seafood and/or ground pork wrapped in rice paper and deep fried. The fried rolls are often served wrapped in lettuce leaves. There is no one recipe for cha-gio. It is said that the Vietnamese consider the ability to make good cha-gio a qualification for a proper bride.

The Thais are particularly fond of presenting their foods artistically, and vegetables are often carved into flowers, leaves, and fishes. Unpeeled cucumbers, carrots, turnips, radishes, and green onions are used to garnish dishes artistically and colorfully.

### Starches: Rice and Noodles

Rice is the staple starch in the Southeast Asian diet. Two types of rice are used: long grain and short grain. Long grain is the more familiar white, fluffy rice served with all meals of the Vietnamese and most Thais. Short grain or glutinous rice is the staple in Laos and Northern Thailand. It is referred to as "sticky rice" and is eaten with the fingers. Glutinous rice is used by all Southeast Asians in their desserts.

Noodles, which no doubt came with the Chinese who migrated to Southeast Asia, are an important part of the Southeast Asian diet. There are many types of noodles: egg noodles, rice noodles, mung bean noodles, and rice vermicelli noodles. Rice vermicelli noodles, also called rice sticks or Chinese rice noodles, are made from glutinous rice. They are sold in bundles packaged in cellophane bags. Dry and brittle in this form, they must be soaked in water before use. They are then combined with meats or vegetables. Sometimes these noodles are deep fried as they come from the package. They puff up and become crisp. The classic Thai salad, mee krob, is made with noodles in this form. Similar to rice vermicelli are mung bean noodles, also called cellophane noodles. These noodles have no flavor of their own, but absorb the flavor of the dish to which they are added.

Wide, flat noodles are also used in Southeast Asian cookery. Noodles such as the Thai gwaytio are often stir-fried with meat and vegetables to create dishes similar to those of the Chinese. A popular Vietnamese soup called pho is also prepared with wide rice noodles. Usually eaten for breakfast or a snack in Vietnam, pho is not often prepared at home but rather bought from street vendors or from pho stands.

### Sweets

Desserts are popular with Southeast Asians, particularly with the Thais. The desserts for the most part tend to be quite sweet and fall into two categories. One category consists of the liquid desserts of fruits and vegetables served in sweetened coconut milk or sugar syrups. The second category consists of sweetmeats, jellied cakes, or steamed puddings of sticky rice. The cakes are often fashioned into miniature fruit shapes or served in cups made out of banana leaves. Others are delicately tinted and cut into diamonds or small squares.

Coconut milk is the main ingredient of many desserts.

Tapioca and glutinous rice are used to thicken the sweetmeats, and they are often delicately flavored with essence of jasmine or rosewater or pounded pandanus leaves. Some desserts of Southeast Asia show a Portuguese influence. Golden threads, a delicate Thai dessert made of egg yolks drizzled in boiling sugar syrup, and egg-rich custards are two desserts borrowed from the Portuguese.

### Celebrations

Like other Orientals, Southeast Asian people celebrate the New Year ceremoniously. They follow the lunar calendar and their New Year coincides with Chinese New Year. Even during the war in Vietnam, Tet, the Vietnamese New Year, was observed by those who could. Families were reunited if possible and traditional holiday foods such as shark fin soup and banana leaf wrapped sticky rice cakes filled with meat and beans were prepared. Southeast Asians who have come to this country celebrate the Western New Year as well as the lunar New Year.

Weddings and birthdays are also celebrated. One Thai sweet which is often served at weddings is *Kanom Sam Kloe*. This is a sweet fritter-like dough made out of sticky rice flour that is dipped in a batter then deep fried. The dough is rolled into small balls and made in groups of three. The attachment of the balls during cooking is supposed to predict the future of the wedding couple. It is believed that if the balls adhere to each other well during cooking, they ensure a happy marriage; if all three balls separate, the marriage is doomed to failure. If one ball breaks away, it is believed that the marriage will be childless. To guarantee a happy marriage, all one has to do is make the batter thick enough for the balls to stick together!

For instructions on how to make fresh coconut milk for these recipes, see the Hawaiian section on coconut milk.

# Ken Som Pa
### Sour Fish Soup - Laotian

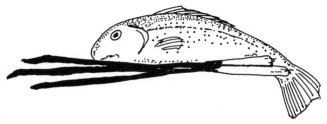

**Serves 4**

   3 c. water
   ½ tsp. salt
   2 stalks fresh lemon grass (or 2 tsp. powdered lemon grass)
   1 large tomato, peeled, seeded, cut into 1-inch pieces
   ½ lb. freshwater fish fillets such as trout or perch cut into 1-inch pieces
   2 Tbsp. fish sauce (nam pla)
   3 stalks green onion, chopped
   2 Tbsp. coriander leaves, chopped
   2 tsp. lime or lemon juice

Combine water and salt in a large saucepan. If using fresh lemon grass, crush the stalks to release flavor; add to the water. Heat water to boiling; reduce heat and simmer 10 minutes. Turn heat to medium and add tomato; cover and cook 10 minutes. Add fish and fish sauce; reduce heat to low and cook, covered, for 10 minutes. Remove and discard lemon grass. Add onions and coriander to soup. Remove from heat. Place ½ tsp. of lemon or lime juice in individual bowls. Ladle soup into bowls and serve at once.

# Cha-Gio
## Vietnamese Spring Roll

**Serves 4-6**

¼ lb. ground pork
¼ lb. raw shrimp or crab
2 carrots
½ tsp. salt
oil for frying

¼ lb. chop suey yam (also known as jicama)
2 stalks green onion, chopped
pepper to taste

triangle or round rice paper wrappers (Chinese spring roll wrappers or Filipino lumpia wrappers may be substituted)

Shred chop suey yam and carrots into matchstick pieces. Remove shell from crab or shrimp. Mash crab or shrimp with ground pork; season with salt and pepper. Mix in carrots, chop suey yam, and green onion. Separate sheets of rice paper wrappers and place approximately 1 Tbsp. of filling in the center. Fold left and right sides over the mixture and then roll into a small, cylindrical package. Deep fry in hot oil until golden brown. Drain on paper towels. Serve hot with leaf lettuce. May be served with or without sauce.

### Sauce:

2 Tbsp. water
2 Tbsp. vinegar
1 Tbsp. sugar

2-3 Tbsp. nuoc mam (fish sauce)
1 clove garlic, finely chopped
½ tsp. red chili pepper, finely chopped

**Note:** Turnips may be substituted for chop suey yam.


# Goi-Ga
## Vietnamese Chicken Salad

**Serves 4-6**

1 lb. shredded head cabbage
1 bunch mint leaves, washed and removed from stems
1 lb. chicken breast, cooked
1 small onion, thinly sliced
1 small carrot, cut in matchstick pieces

Shred the cooked chicken meat. In a large bowl, combine chicken with vegetables and mint leaves. Pour dressing over and let stand 10 minutes before serving.

### Dressing:

| | |
|---|---|
| 1 tsp. sugar | 2 cloves garlic, mashed |
| 1 Tbsp. oil | ¼ c. rice vinegar or lime juice |
| finely chopped red chili pepper to taste | |

# Kai Yat Sai
## Pork Stuffed Omelets - Thai

**Serves 4-6**

| | |
|---|---|
| 8 peppercorns | 3 cloves garlic, chopped |
| 4 Tbsp. vegetable oil | 2 tsp. coriander roots, chopped |
| ½ c. ground pork | ½ c. Chinese peas, chopped |
| 1 small onion, chopped | 1 medium tomato, chopped |
| 1 tsp. sugar | 1 Tbsp. fish sauce (nam pla) |
| 8 eggs, beaten | 2 Tbsp. coriander leaves |

With a mortar and pestle, grind together the garlic, peppercorns, and coriander roots into a paste. Heat 2 Tbsp. of the oil in a frying pan and fry the paste for 2 minutes. Add the pork and stir-fry until brown. Add onion, peas, and tomato and stir-fry 1 minute. Stir in the sugar and set pork mixture aside.

Beat eggs with the fish sauce. Heat 1 Tbsp. oil in an omelet pan or frying pan. Pour in half of the egg mixture. Spoon in half of the pork mixture down the center of the omelet. Allow eggs to set and fold omelet over. Slide onto a plate. Repeat process with the other half of the eggs and pork. Cut omelets in serving pieces and garnish with coriander leaves.

# Mawk Mak Phet
### Steamed Stuffed Chili Peppers - Laotian

**Serves 5**

10 large fresh chili peppers such as poblanos
2 Tbsp. glutinous rice    4 large shallots, crushed to a paste
1 lb. ground pork          3 stalks green onion, finely chopped
¼ tsp. black pepper        2 Tbsp. fish sauce (nam pla)
banana leaves, washed and dried

Soak rice in a bowl of cold water for 1 hour. Drain; grind in a
blender or pound in mortar and pestle until particles are the size
of coarse meal. Make a pocket in each chili pepper by slitting
from one side from stem to tip with a paring knife, being careful
not to cut through other side. Remove seeds under running water.
Soak chilies in a bowl of cold water for 30 minutes.

Drain and dry with paper towels. Combine pork, shallots,
green onions, ground rice, fish sauce, and pepper in a bowl. Mix
thoroughly. Stuff each chili with pork mixture. Wrap chilies in
banana leaves, two to a packet. Secure with string. (If banana
leaves are not available use foil.)

Arrange packets in a steamer. Cover and steam over boiling
water for 25 minutes, or until pork is no longer pink.

# Boiled Chicken with Jaew Som
## Laotian

**Serves 4-6**

| | |
|---|---|
| 3 c. water | 1 lb. carrots, pared and cut in half |
| 1 chicken, about 3 lbs. | 1 daikon, pared and cut into wedges |
| ½ tsp. salt | 2 bulbs kohlrabi, pared, quartered |
| 3 stalks coriander | 2 stalks celery, cut into 1-inch pieces |
| 1 onion, cut in wedges | 4 stalks green onions, chopped |

1 Tbsp. fish sauce (nam pla)
1 small head cauliflower, separated into flowerets
finely chopped coriander and green onion for garnish

Heat water in soup pot or Dutch oven to boiling. Add chicken and salt; cover. Reduce heat to medium and simmer 20 minutes. Sprinkle with fish sauce. Add carrots, daikon, kohlrabi, and coriander; simmer, covered, 15 minutes. Add celery, cauliflower, onion, and green onions; simmer for 15 minutes or until chicken and vegetables are tender.

With a slotted spoon, remove vegetables to the outside edges of a deep platter. Remove chicken, cut into serving pieces and arrange in the center of the platter. Sprinkle with black pepper and garnish with coriander and green onion. Serve chicken and vegetables in soup plates with a small amount of broth ladled over each serving. Serve with Jaew Som.

### Jaew Som:

| | |
|---|---|
| 1 Tbsp. fish sauce | 10 cloves garlic, finely chopped |
| 4 dried red chili peppers | 1 tsp. finely chopped coriander leaves |

Place chilies under broiler and char, turning frequently until they are brittle (1-2 minutes). Cool, discard stems, crumble chilies. Pound chilies with the rest of the ingredients in mortar and pestle until it reaches a paste-like consistency. Refrigerate until ready to serve.

# Satay
## Cooking on Skewers - Thai

**Serves 4-6**

1 lb. beef, pork, or chicken, thinly sliced into strips ½" x 2"

| **Marinade:** | **Sauce:** |
|---|---|
| 2 cloves garlic, minced | ½ c. crunchy peanut butter |
| ½ onion, chopped | 1 onion, finely chopped |
| 1 Tbsp. brown sugar | 1 c. coconut milk |
| juice of 1 lime | 1 Tbsp. brown sugar |
| 1 Tbsp. fish sauce (nam pla) | 1 Tbsp. soy sauce |
| 1 Tbsp. vegetable oil | 1 tsp. cayenne |
| | 1 Tbsp. fish sauce (nam pla) |
| | 1 stalk lemon grass, chopped |

Place the ingredients of the marinade in a blender or food processor and process until smooth. Thread the meat like a ribbon on 12" wooden skewers and place them in a shallow pan. Pour marinade over the meat and let stand for 1 hour, turning occasionally. Grill the meat over coals or under a broiler.

In a saucepan, combine all the sauce ingredients and bring to a boil, stirring. Remove from heat and pour into bowls. Dip meat into sauce, or pour sauce over the skewers of meat.

# Takaw
## Tapioca-Coconut Creams - Thai

**Makes 16-20**

| | |
|---|---|
| ½ c. tapioca flour | 2 Tbsp. rice flour |
| 6 Tbsp. sugar | 1 c. coconut milk |
| 1⅓ c. water | dash of salt |
| 1 tsp rosewater | |

In a bowl, mix the tapioca flour, sugar and water until the mixture is smooth. Strain mixture through damp muslin or cheesecloth into a medium sized saucepan. Heat the mixture over medium heat until it thickens and becomes clear. Remove from heat and add the rosewater. Pour into small, fluted paper or foil cups, filling each about one half full. Place the cups on a cookie sheet and refrigerate while preparing the next layer.

In a clean saucepan, blend the rice flour with the coconut milk, stirring until the mixture is smooth. Add salt; place the pan over low heat and stir constantly until the mixture thickens. Remove the cups from the refrigerator and pour the coconut custard layer over the first layer. Refrigerate 1-2 hours or until firm.

**Note:** In Thailand, these sweets are sold in individual containers made out of banana leaves.

# Pork and Vegetable Curry
## Thai

**Serves 4**

½ c. vegetable oil
3 Tbsp. red curry paste (krung gaeng ped)
1 c. lean pork, cut into thin slices ½" x 2"
2 Tbsp. fish sauce (nam pla)
1 stalk lemon grass, chopped
½ c. cabbage, chopped
½ c. green beans, cut in 1½" pieces
1 c. dried Chinese mushrooms, soaked in hot water and cut into strips
4 fresh red Serrano chilies, seeded and cut into strips
2 tsp. sugar
12 mint leaves, chopped

Heat oil in frying pan and fry the red curry paste for 3 minutes, stirring until color and odor change. Add pork, fish sauce, and lemon grass. Stir-fry for 5 minutes. Add cabbage, beans, and mushrooms. Sprinkle with chili strips and sugar and fry for 1 minute. Remove to a serving bowl and garnish with mint leaves.

# Coconut-Sesame Seed Dumplings
## Vietnamese

**Serves 6-8**

### Filling:

3 Tbsp. toasted sesame seeds
1 fresh coconut, grated (or 1½ c. baker's coconut)
1 c. sugar (½ c. if using sweetened coconut)
1 c. water

Toast sesame seeds in heavy skillet for 3-5 minutes. Remove meat from coconut and grate. Toast in heavy skillet over medium heat for 2 minutes. Add sugar and water to coconut and continue stirring and cooking for about 3 minutes. Add sesame seeds and continue to stir and cook another 3 minutes over medium heat. Cool.

### Dough:

¾ c. water
¼ c. sugar
10 oz. mochiko (glutinous rice flour)

Mix water and sugar together in saucepan; bring to a boil, stirring until sugar is dissolved. Remove from heat and cool.

Mix the sugar and water with the mochiko. Put a drop of cooking oil in the palm of the hands and pinch off enough dough to form a ball about 1 inch in diameter. Roll dough until a smooth ball is formed. Then flatten it, making a circle about 3 inches across. Put a teaspoonful of coconut-sesame filling in the center, pinch together and form a ball again. Drop the balls into hot cooking oil and fry until golden brown. Drain on absorbent towels. Serve hot.

# Kanom Sam Kloe
## Three Chum Cakes - Thai

**Serves 6**

### Sweetmeats:

6 Tbsp. mochiko (glutinous rice flour)

¼ c. mung beans, dry roasted until brown and ground in mortar or blender to make a fine flour

cold water

1 c. sweetened shredded coconut

½ c. sesame seeds

4 Tbsp. palm sugar (or substitute 2 Tbsp. brown sugar and 2 Tbsp. molasses)

In a saucepan mix together flour and mung bean powder with enough water to form a paste for consistency of heavy cream. Stir in coconut, sesame seeds, and sugar. Add more water if needed. Place pan over low heat, stir until thickened and dough is solid enough to roll into balls. Remove pan from heat, cool until you can handle it, and roll into small balls, about ½ inch in diameter.

### Batter:

| | |
|---|---|
| 1 egg beaten | ¾ c. rice flour (or all purpose flour) |
| ¼ tsp. salt | vegetable oil for deep frying |
| ¼ c. coconut milk | |

Mix all ingredients together to form a thick batter. Heat oil in a wok or heavy pan to 375 degrees. Dip the balls in the batter and deep fry them in groups of three until crisp and golden brown. Drain on absorbent paper. Serve warm.

**Note:** Served at weddings

# Glossary

## A

**Aburage:** *(Japanese)* deep-fried tofu.

**Acorda:** Portuguese bread soup.

**Achara:** Filipino pickled vegetables or fruit.

**Achiote seeds:** seeds of the annatto or lipstick tree used in Filipino and Puerto Rican cookery to achieve a reddish color in foods.

**Adobo:** Filipino dish of pork, chicken, or other meat simmered in vinegar, garlic, and spices.

**Aemono:** Japanese vegetable dish consisting of lightly cooked vegetables in dressing.

**Agemono:** *(Japanese)* Fried food.

**'Ahi:** *(Hawaiian)* Yellow fin tuna.

**'Ai noa:** *(Hawaiian)* to eat without observance of kapu.

**'Aina:** *(Hawaiian)* land or earth.

**'Akala:** Hawaiian raspberry.

**Aku:** *(Hawaiian)* a young tuna known also as bonito or skipjack.

**Akua:** *(Hawaiian)* a god.

**'Alae:** *(Hawaiian)* mudhen.

**Annatto seeds:** *see* achiote seeds.

**Apritada:** *(Filipino)* Pork with pimento and garbanzo beans

**Arroz con coco:** *(Puerto Rican)* Coconut rice pudding.

**Arroz con pollo:** Puerto Rican dish of chicken with rice.

**Arroz doce:** Portuguese sweet rice.

**'Aumakua:** *(Hawaiian)* family god.

**Azuki:** red beans used in Japanese cookery.

## B

**Bacalao:** *(Puerto Rican)* codfish.

**Bacalhau:** *(Portuguese)* codfish.

**Bagoong:** fish paste used in flavoring Filipino dishes.

**Balatong:** *(Filipino)* Mungo beans and pork.

**Bibinka:** Filipino dessert made out of mochiko, sugar, coconut milk.

**Bitter melon:** green spiny vegetable of the gourd family with a slightly bitter taste.

**Black Beans:** Fermented beans with salty flavor used in Chinese cookery.

**Braoas:** *(Portuguese)* Round cakes similar to sugar cookies.

**Broa:** Portuguese cornbread.

**Bul kogi:** *(Korean)* Thin slices of barbecued beef.

**Bulo do mel:** *(Portuguese)* honey cakes.

**Bunuelos:** Filipino dumplings, fried then rolled in sugar.

## C

**Calabash:** bowl used by Hawaiians, usually large.

**Caldeirada:** Portuguese seafood stew.

**Caldo verde:** Portuguese cabbage and bean (or potato) soup.

**Cellophane noodles:** see long rice.

**Chap chae:** (Korean) Stir-fried dish of vegetables, meat, and noodles.

**Char siu:** (Chinese) sweet flavored roast pork.

**Chicharrones:** (Puerto Rican) deep-fried pork rind.

**Chick pea:** legume related to garden pea; available dried or canned. Also known as garbanzo beans.

**Chili oil:** oil flavored with red chilies.

**Chinese parsley:** see coriander.

**Chop suey:** stir fried dish of meat and vegetables.

**Chorizo:** a hot and spicy Portuguese sausage.

**Chun:** (Korean) Foods fried in an egg batter.

**Chung Choy:** Chinese preserved turnip.

**Cilantro:** see coriander.

**Coriander:** pungent herb, member of the parsley family, used in Oriental, Latin American, and Italian dishes. Also known as Chinese parsley or cilantro.

**Creche:** Nativity scene.

**D**

**Dai-dai:** Japanese citrus fruit similar to a tangerine.

**Daikon:** Oriental radish; a large, white root vegetable.

**Dashi:** (Japanese) seasoned soup base or broth.

**Dim sum:** general name given to Chinese dumplings filled with meat or sweets. Also known as manapua in Hawai'i.

**D'ok guk:** Korean New Year's soup.

**Dow foo:** Chinese for tofu; see tofu.

**E**

**Esi fafao** (Samoan) stuffed papaya.

**F**

**Five-spice powder:** Combination of star anise, cloves, fennel, cinnamon, and peppercorns; a seasoning in Chinese cooking.

**Fornos tejollos:** traditional Portuguese ovens, commonly known as fornos.

**Fu young:** (Chinese) mixed up, scrambled; e.g. egg fu young.

**G**

**Galingale:** rhizome of the ginger family used in Southeast Asian cookery; also called ka.

**Gandul:** (Puerto Rican) see pigeon peas.

**Garbanzo beans:** see chick peas.

**Gau:** Chinese sweet rice cake, most often made at New Year's.

**Ginger Root:** A root which adds spicy flavor to many Oriental dishes; available fresh at most supermarkets.

**Gobo:** *(Japanese)* burdock root.

**Goi-ga:** Vietnamese chicken salad.

**Guava:** Tropical fruit with thick rind, soft pulp, many seeds; used mainly for its juice.

**Guinataan:** Filipino pudding made out of coconut milk, yams, taro, and bananas.

**Gwaytio:** *(Thai)* wide, flat noodles.

# H

**Hākui:** *(Hawaiian)* to steam by placing food in a calabash with hot stones and water.

**Hale 'aina:** *(Hawaiian)* eating house reserved for women.

**Hale mua:** *(Hawaiian)* men's eating house.

**Halo-halo:** Filipino liquid dessert of milk, ice, sugar, and various fruits.

**Hāpu'u:** Hawaiian tree fern.

**Harm har:** Chinese seasoning made out of fermented shrimp.

**Haupia:** *(Hawaiian)* Coconut pudding.

**Hawaiian salt:** coarse salt, rock salt.

# I

**Ichogiri:** *(Japanese)* method of cutting vegetables in crosswise slices, then quartering the slices.

**Imu:** *(Hawaiian)* underground oven.

# J

**Jai:** A traditional vegetarian dish served at Chinese New Year; also known as monk's food.

**Jook:** *(Chinese)* rice gruel.

# K

**Ka:** *see* galingale.

**Kai yat sai:** *(Thai)* omelet with pork.

**Kalamansi:** Filipino lime

**Kalbi:** Korean style short ribs.

**Kale:** green vegetable of the cabbage family; also known as Portuguese cabbage.

**Kalo:** Hawaiian word for taro.

**Kālua:** *(Hawaiian)* To bake in an underground oven.

**Kālua pig:** whole pig cooked in an underground oven.

**Kamaboko:** Japanese seasoned fishcake.

**Kampyo:** *(Japanese)* Dried flesh of bottle gourd; used in making sushi.

**Kang jang:** *(Korean)* flavored soy sauce.

**Kanten:** Japanese gelatin dessert made out of agar-agar (seaweed).

**Kapa:** Hawaiian bark cloth, also known as tapa.

**Kapu:** ancient Hawaiian law; system of restriction.

**Katsuobushi:** dried bonito flakes used as a seasoning in Japanese foods.

**Kazali:** Japanese New Year's altar offering for good luck.

**Kazunoko:** *(Japanese)* herring roe.

**Kim chee:** Korean pickled vegetables with hot, spicy flavor.

**Kimpira:** *(Japanese)* a dish made out of burdock root, shoyu, and sugar.

**Kō'ala:** *(Hawaiian)* method of broiling over hot coals.

**Kochu jang:** thick Korean hot sauce.

**Kogi guk:** Korean beef soup.

**Koko:** *see* tsukemono.

**Kōlea:** *(Hawaiian)* plover.

**Kōloa:** *(Hawaiian)* wild duck.

**Konbu:** *(Japanese)* seaweed.

**Konnyaku:** *(Japanese)* Firm, jelly-like substance made from tuber called devil's tongue. Sold in blocks or in noodle form called shirataki.

**Kook Soo:** *(Korean)* Noodles in broth, served hot or cold and garnished with meat and vegetables.

**Kūlolo:** *(Hawaiian)* taro pudding.

**Kūmū:** *(Hawaiian)* goatfish.

**Kuri:** *(Japanese)* chestnut.

**Kuromame:** Japanese black beans; a traditional New Year's food.

### L

**Lapinha:** Portuguese nativity scene.

**Laulau:** *(Hawaiian)* taro leaves (lū'au), pork, and salted fish wrapped in ti leaves and traditionally cooked in an imu.

**Laver:** thin sheets of seaweed used in Korean cookery.

**Lechon asado:** *(Puerto Rican)* roast suckling pig.

**Lemon grass:** herb with long green leaves with a sour flavor used in Southeast Asian cookery; also called citronella.

**Limu:** *(Hawaiian)* seaweed.

**Linguica:** hot, spicy Portuguese sausage.

**Lomi:** *(Hawaiian)* to squeeze, crush, or mash.

**Long rice:** dried, transparent noodles made out of mung bean starch. Also known as cellophane noodles.

**Lū'au:** a Hawaiian feast.

**Lū'au** (leaves): *(Hawaiian)* green tops of the taro plant.

**Lumpia:** Filipino vegetable-meat roll, deep fried. Similar to spring roll.

**Lup chong:** spicy Chinese sausage.

### M

**Mai'a:** *(Hawaiian)* Banana or banana plant.

**Makahiki:** Hawaiian holiday season of thanksgiving; originally spanning four months for the chiefs.

**Malassadas:** Portuguese doughnuts.

**Manapua:** *see* dim sum.

**Mandu:** Korean dumplings filled with chopped meat and vegetables.

**Manju:** *(Japanese)* small bun filled with sweet bean paste.

**Marungay:** leaves of the horse-radish tree used in Filipino cookery.

**Massa sovada:** Portuguese Easter bread with eggs baked on top.

**Mawk mak phet:** (*Laotian*) stuffed chili peppers.

**Mee krob:** Thai salad with fried noodles.

**Mein:** (*Chinese*) noodles.

**Mirin:** Japanese sweet rice wine.

**Miso:** fermented soybean paste.

**Moa:** (*Hawaiian*) domesticated fowl similar to chicken used by Hawaiians as food.

**Mochi:** Japanese rice cakes traditionally made at New Year's.

**Mochiko:** (*Japanese*) glutinous rice flour; mochi rice flour.

**Monk's food:** *see* jai.

**Morcela:** Portuguese blood sausage.

**Mung beans:** small greenish brown beans used to produce bean sprouts.

**Mushimono:** (*Japanese*) steamed foods.

**Musubi:** Japanese rice ball.

### N

**Nabemono:** (*Japanese*) one-pot dishes.

**Nam pla:** Thai fish sauce.

**Nam prik:** Thai hot sauce.

**Namasu:** Japanese salad consisting of vegetables in vinegar sauce.

**Namul:** (*Korean*) slightly cooked vegetables in a sauce of sesame seeds, oil, vinegar, and soy sauce.

**Nēnē:** Hawaiian goose.

**Nimono:** (*Japanese*) foods simmered in a liquid.

**Nishime:** Japanese vegetable dish with bits of pork or chicken.

**Nori:** (*Japanese*) seaweed.

**Nuoc mam:** Vietnamese fish sauce.

**Nurm juk:** (*Korean*) meat, kim chee, and vegetables on skewers.

### O

**Ogo:** common name for species of seaweed known in Hawai‘i as limu manauea.

**‘Ohana:** (*Hawaiian*) Offshoot of the taro corm; family social unit.

**‘Ohelo:** Hawaiian plant with edible berries.

**Okara:** (*Japanese*) tofu derivative; the residue after soy milk has been pressed out of soybeans.

**Okazu-ya:** Japanese delicatessen.

**‘Opakapaka:** (*Hawaiian*) pink snapper.

**‘Opihi:** (*Hawaiian*) limpets.

**Oyster sauce:** Chinese seasoning made out of fermented oysters.

**Ozoni:** soup with mochi and vegetables traditionally eaten by Japanese on New Year's day.

### P

**Padek:** Laotian fish sauce.

**Paella:** casserole of rice, meat, seafood, and vegetables; Spanish in origin.

**Palu sami:** *(Samoan)* taro leaves in coconut cream.

**Pansit:** Filipino noodles.

**Pao doce:** Portuguese sweet bread.

**Pasteles:** *(Puerto Rican)* bananas stuffed with pork.

**Pastelillos:** *(Puerto Rican)* Fried pork turnovers.

**Patis:** liquid fish sauce used in flavoring Filipino dishes.

**Pe'e pe'e:** Samoan coconut cream.

**Pho:** a Vietnamese soup.

**Pigeon peas:** a tropical legume used by Puerto Ricans; known also as gandul.

**Pinacbet:** Filipino cooked vegetable dish flavored with shrimp or pork.

**Pipi kaula:** Hawaiian style beef jerky.

**Plantain:** cooking bananas.

**Plum sauce:** Sweet, spicy sauce used for dipping Chinese foods.

**Pochero:** Filipino casserole of meat, vegetables, chickpeas, and potatoes.

**Poi:** staple starch of Hawaiians made out of taro.

**Poi 'ulu:** *(Hawaiian, Samoan)* breadfruit poi.

**Poke:** *(Hawaiian)* to slice crosswise into pieces; food made in that way such as "aku poke."

**Polvorones:** *(Puerto Rican)* a kind of cookie.

**Ponque:** *(Puerto Rican)* pound cake.

**Pōpolo:** *(Hawaiian)* Plant of the tomato family with edible berries and leaves.

**Povi masima:** *(Samoan)* salt beef brisket.

**Pudim flan:** *(Portuguese)* custard.

**Pūholo:** *(Hawaiian)* to steam (food), expecially by stuffing flesh with hot rocks and placing in a covered calabash.

**Pūlehu:** *(Hawaiian)* method of broiling over hot ashes.

## R

**Rangiri:** *(Japanese)* a method of cutting vegetables on a diagonal, turning, and cutting on the other diagonal.

**Rhizome:** an underground rootlike stem that grows horizontally, often thickened with stored food.

**Rice vinegar:** Japanese vinegar; milder than Western vinegars.

## S

**Sabula de vinha:** Portuguese pickled onions.

**Sancocho:** Puerto Rican vegetable stew.

**Saengsun chun:** Korean fried fish.

**Sangchu sam:** Korean rice ball seasoned with hot sauce and wrapped in a lettuce leaf.

**Sasagaki:** *(Japanese)* method of cutting vegetables into slivers.

**Sashimi:** *(Japanese)* sliced raw fish.

**Satay:** Cooking on skewers.

**Sekihan:** Japanese rice and red bean (azuki) dish.

**Senbei:** Japanese sweet rice crackers.

**Serenata:** (*Puerto Rican*) Codfish salad.

**Sesame oil:** oil made out of sesame seeds; used as a flavoring in Oriental dishes.

**Shabu-shabu:** Japanese dish of meat and/or seafood and vegetables cooked in simmering broth.

**Shallot:** a small onion-like vegetable.

**Shira ae:** vegetables, tofu, and dressing; a Japanese salad.

**Shirataki:** see Konnyaku.

**Shoyu:** Japanese word for soy sauce.

**Sin choy:** Chinese preserved mustard cabbage.

**Sinigang:** Filipino soup made with fish, shrimp or meat and vegetables.

**Sinsollo:** (*Korean*) meats and vegetables cooked in a broth.

**Soba:** buckwheat noodles, traditionally eaten by Japanese on New Year's eve.

**Sofrito:** Puerto Rican tomato sauce.

**Somen:** (*Japanese*) thin wheat noodles.

**Songphyun:** Korean pastry filled with bean paste or sesame seed filling.

**Sopa borrocha:** Puerto Rican sponge cake with rum sauce.

**Soupa de feijaos:** Portuguese bean soup.

**Spoon meat:** soft flesh of a young coconut.

**Spring roll:** see cha-gio.

**Star anise:** small, dried, licorice-flavored spice used in Chinese cooking.

**Stir fry:** method of cooking quickly over high heat in a small amount of oil.

**Sudare:** (*Japanese*) Bamboo mat used for rolling sushi.

**Sukiyaki:** Japanese dish of meat and vegetables in shoyu based sauce.

**Suribachi:** Japanese mortar and pestle.

**Sushi:** rice seasoned with vinegar sauce.

**Sushi bar:** Japanese restaurant that serves different varieties of sushi.

**Sweet Bean Paste:** thick paste made out of red beans, used as a filling for Oriental pastries.

## T

**Taegu:** Korean seasoned dried codfish or cuttlefish.

**Tai:** Sea bream, a large red fish.

**Takaw:** (*Thai*) Tapioca-coconut creams.

**Takuwan:** Japanese pickled daikon or turnip.

**Talo:** (*Samoan*) see taro.

**Tamarind:** tree which produces edible pods with a sour flavor.

**Taro:** A starchy tuber; a staple of Hawaiians.

**Taufolo:** Samoan dish of mashed breadfruit and coconut milk.

**Tempura:** *(Japanese)* Food dipped in batter and fried.

**Teriyaki:** A Japanese dish consisting of meats marinated in a soy sauce mixture then grilled.

**Thousand year old eggs:** *(Chinese)* Duck eggs coated with lime, clay, salt, ashes, in reality only four or five months old.

**Tofu:** soybean curd.

**Tremocos:** salted lupine seeds; a Portuguese snack food.

**Tsukemono:** Japanese pickled vegetables.

**Tupig:** Filipino dessert made out of mochiko and coconut milk, wrapped in banana leaves.

## U

**'Uala:** *(Hawaiian)* sweet potato.

**'Uala 'awa'awa:** *(Hawaiian)* Sweet potato beer.

**Udon:** *(Japanese)* thick wheat noodles.

**Uhi:** *(Hawaiian)* yam.

**'Ulu:** *(Hawaiian)* Breadfruit.

**Ulua:** *(Hawaiian)* certain species of jack, an important fish for food.

**'Umeke:** Hawaiian food bowl; calabash.

**Umu:** Samoan outdoor oven.

## V

**Vinha d'alhos:** *(Portuguese)* Fish or meat marinated in a wine vinegar, and garlic mixture before cooking.

## W

**Water chestnut:** small crunchy tuber used in Oriental cookery.

**Wok:** pan with curved bottom and sides used in Chinese and other Oriental cookery.

**Won ton:** Chinese dumplings filled with ground pork; may be deep fried or in soup.

## Y

**Yak kwa:** *(Korean)* deep fried dessert rolled in honey.

**Yak pahb:** Korean dessert of sweet mochi rice, pinenuts, chestnuts, sesame seeds, and dried fruit. Also known as "yak sik."

**Yak sik:** *see* yak phab.

**Yakimono:** *(Japanese)* broiled or grilled foods.

**Yaki tori kushi:** *(Japanese)* chicken on a stick.

**Yautia:** a type of taro used in Puerto Rican cookery.

**Yokan:** Japanese sweet made out of sweet bean paste.

# Bibliography

Anderson, Anne. "The Many Pleasures of Puerto Rico." *Cuisine,* January 1982, pp. 37-44.

Arroyo, Patricia. *The Science of Philippine Foods.* Quezon City, Philippines: Abaniko Enterprises, 1974.

Bazore, Katherine. *Hawaiian and Pacific Foods.* New York: Barrows, 1947.

Brennan, Jennifer. *The Original Thai Cookbook.* New York: Richard Marek Publishers, 1981.

Brooks, Karen. *The Global Kitchen.* New York: Andrews and McMeel, 1981.

Buck, Sir Peter H. *Arts and Crafts of Hawaii.* Vol. 1. Honolulu: Bishop Museum Press, 1964.

Buck, Sir Peter H. *Samoan Material Culture.* Honolulu: Bishop Museum Press, 1930.

Cabinallas, Berta. *Puerto Rican Dishes.* Rio Peidras: University of Puerto Rico, 1974.

Chang, K.C. *Food in Chinese Culture: Anthropological and Historical Perspectives.* New Haven, Connecticut: Yale University Press, 1977.

Char, Stephanie Ayers. "Lapinha; a Portuguese Christmas Tradition." *Honolulu,* December 1977, pp. 41-44.

Choi, E. Soon Yim. *Practical Korean Recipes.* Seoul, Korea: Yonsei University Press, 1977.

Chung, May Lee. *Traditions for Living: a Booklet of Chinese Customs and Folk Practices in Hawaii.* Honolulu: Associated Chinese University Women, 1979.

Davidson, Alan. "The Traditions of Laos." *Cuisine,* May 1982, pp. 43-45, 82-89.

Daws, Gavan. *The Shoal of Time.* Honolulu: University of Hawaii Press, 1974.

Dunford, Betty. *The Hawaiians of Old.* Honolulu: The Bess Press, 1980.

Ellis, William. *Polynesian Researches: Hawaii.* Tokyo, Japan: Charles E. Tuttle, 1969.

Feher, Joseph. *Hawaii: A Pictorial History.* Honolulu: Bishop Museum Press, 1969.

Feibleman, Peter S. *The Cooking of Spain and Portugal.* New York: Time-Life, 1969.

Felix, John Henry, *Portuguese in Hawaii,* Honolulu: Felix, 1978.

Fortner, Heather. *The Limu Eater, a Cookbook of Hawaiian Seaweed.* Honolulu: University of Hawaii Sea Grant Miscellaneous Report 79-01, 1978.

Goldman, Irving. *Ancient Polynesian Society.* Chicago: University of Chicago Press, 1970.

Hahn, Emily. *The Cooking of China.* New York: Time-Life, 1973.

Handy, E.S. Craighill. *Ancient Hawaiian Civilization.* Tokyo, Japan: Charles E. Tuttle, 1965.

Handy, E.S. Craighill and Elizabeth Gree Handy. *Native Planters in Old Hawaii, Their Life, Lore, and Environment.* Honolulu: Bishop Museum Press, 1972.

Handy, E.S. Craighill and Pukui, Mary Kawena. *The Polynesian Family System in Ka'u Hawai'i.* Rutland, Vermont: Charles E. Tuttle, 1972.

*A History of Japanese in Hawaii.* Honolulu: United Japanese Society, 1981.

Hyun, Judy. *The Korean Cookbook.* Chicago, Illinois: Follett, 1970.

Koehler, Margaret H. *Recipes from the Portuguese of Provincetown.* Riverside, Connecticut: The Chatham Press, 1973.

Malo, David. *Hawaiian Antiquities.* Honolulu: Bishop Museum Press, 1951.

Melendy, Howard Brett. *Asians in America: Filipinos, Koreans, and East Asians.* Boston, Massachusetts: Twayne Publishers, 1977.

Miller, Carey D. *Fruits of Hawaii.* Honolulu: University of Hawaii Press, 1965.

Mullins, Joseph G. *Hawaiian Journey.* Honolulu: Mutual Publishing Co., 1978.

Multi-Cultural Center. *Portuguese in Hawaii; a Resource Guide.* Honolulu: Ethnic Research and Resource Center, 1973.

Murai, Mary. *Some Tropical South Pacific Island Foods: Description, History, Use, Composition, and Nutritive Value.* Honolulu: University of Hawaii Press, 1958.

Neal, Marie C. *In Gardens of Hawaii.* Honolulu: Bishop Museum Press, 1965.

Nicholson, Barbara Evelyn. *The Oxford Book of Food Plants.* London, England: Oxford University Press, 1965.

Ok, Cho Joong. *Home Style Korean Cooking.* Tokyo, Japan: Japan Publications, 1981.

Omae, Kinjiro. *The Book of Sushi.* Tokyo, Japan: Kodansha International, 1981.

Ortiz, Elizabeth Lambert. *The Complete Book of Japanese Cooking.* New York: M. Evans and Co., 1976.

Pap, Leo. *The Portuguese Americans.* Boston, Massachusetts: Twayne Publishers, 1981.

Pukui, Mary Kawena and Elbert, Samuel. *Hawaiian Dicitionary.* Honolulu: University of Hawaii Press, 1971.

*Samoan Resource Book For Teachers.* Honolulu: Department of Education, 1980.

Shenton, James P. *American Cooking: The Melting Pot.* New York: Time-Life, 1971.

Shurtleff, William. *The Book of Miso.* Soquel, California: Autumn Press, 1976.

Steinberg, Rafael. *The Cooking of Japan.* New York: Time-Life, 1970.

Stewart, Charles Samuel. *Journal of a Residence in the Sandwich Islands.* Honolulu: University of Hawaii Press, 1970.

Tannahill, Reay. *Food in History.* New York: Stein and Day, 1973.

Titcomb, Margaret. *Native Use of Fish in Hawaii.* New Plymouth, New Zealand: Avery Press, 1952.

*We Japanese: Being Descriptions of Many of the Customs, Manners, Ceremonies, Festivals, Arts, and Crafts of the Japanese.* Miyanoshita Hakone, Japan: Fujiya Hotel, 1950.

*The World Atlas of Food.* New York: Simon and Shuster, 1974.

Young, Nancy Foon, ed. *Montage: An Ethnic History of Women in Hawaii.* Honolulu: College of Education, University of Hawaii, 1977.

Yu, Eui-Young, ed. *Koreans in Los Angeles: Prospects and Promises.* Los Angeles, California: Center for Korean-American Studies, Cal State Los Angeles, 1982.

# INDEX
## by Ethnic Group

155

# INDEX

sticks, soba, somen, udon
Nrum juk, 94
Nuoc mam, 127

## O

Octopus in coconut milk, 122
'Ohana, 7
Okara, 44
Okazu-ya, 41-42
Oven kālua pig, 15
Oyster sauce, 27
Oyster sauce beef and Chinese peas, 37
Ozoni, 50, 52

## P

Padek, 127
Paella, 85
Palu sami, 116, 121
Pao doce, 60, 64
Papaya, 10, 106
Pasteles, 80, 83
Pastelillos, 77, 86
Patis, 103, 105
Pe'e, pe'e, 120
Pescado en escabeche, 84
Pickled daikon, 45, 54
Pickled fish: Portuguese, 70, Puerto Rican, 84
Pickled pork, 72
Pig, as used by Hawaiians, 5-6
Pig, kālua, 2, 6, 15
Pigeon peas, 76, 79
Pinacbet, 111
Pineapple, 10
Pipi kaula, 15
Plantain, 77, 80
Pochero, 111
Poi, 6-7

Poi bread, 18
Poi 'ulu, 10
Poke, 6, 14
Pork and vegetable curry, 139
Pork, kālua, 2, 6, 15
Pork stuffed omelets, 135
Pork turnovers, 77, 86
Pork with pimento and garbanzo beans, 112
Portuguese bean soup, 65, 70
Portuguese cornbread, 73
Portuguese food and food customs, 60-75
Portuguese pickled fish, 70
Portuguese pickled onions, 69
Portuguese sausage, 61
Portuguese sweet doughnuts, 60, 74
Povi masima, 115, 123
Puerto Rican food and food customs, 76-87

## R

Raw fish, Samoan style, 122
Raw fish with seaweed, 14
Rice, glutinous, 50, 125-126, 130-131
Rice in: Chinese diet, 30, Filipino diet, 106, Japanese diet, 48-49, Korean diet, 93, Portuguese diet 63, Puerto Rican diet, 79, Southeast Asian diet, 130-131
Rice sticks, 131
Rice with chicken, 78, 84

## S

Sabula de vinha, 69
Saengsun chun, 98

93, 101, Portuguese, 63, 74-75, Puerto Rican, 80, 87, Southeast Asian, 131-132, 140-141

Szechwan (cooking style), 21

# T

Taegu, 97
Tai, 51
Takaw, 138
Takuwan, 45, 54
Tapioca coconut creams, 138
Taro, 6-7
Taro leaves baked in coconut cream, 121
Taro pudding, 19
Tea, 32
Tempura, 55
Thai food and food customs see Southeast Asian food and food customs
Thousand year old eggs, 28
Three chum cakes, 141
Three Kings Day, 81
Tofu, 25-26, 43-44
Trigo, 67-68
Tsukemono, 41, 45, 54

# U

Udon, 49
Uhi see yam
'Ulu see breadfruit
Umani see Nishime
'Umeke, 2
Umu, 115

# V

Vegetable stew, 85
Vegetables and shrimp, 111
Vegetables, varieties used by: Chinese, 28, 29, Filipinos, 105, 106, Hawaiians, 11, 12, Japanese, 45, 46, Koreans, 91, 92, Portuguese, 63, Puerto Ricans, 78, 79, Samoans, 116, Southeast Asians, 130
Vietnamese chicken salad, 134
Vietnamese spring roll, 134
Vietnamese food and food customs see Southeast Asian food and food customs
Vinha d'alhos, 61, 72

# W

Watercress-tofu salad, 54
White Sunday, 119
Winter melon soup, 29
Won bok and pork soup, 34
Won ton, 30, 35

# Y

Yak kwa, 94
Yak pahb (honey rice), 101
Yak sik see yak phab
Yaki tori kushi, 56
Yam, 11-12
Yautia, 76
Yokan, 49